BEDOUIN OF THE LONDON EVENING

Rosemary Tonks, *c.* 1968 (photo: Michael Peters)

ROSEMARY TONKS

Bedouin of the London Evening

COLLECTED POEMS

& SELECTED PROSE

BLOODAXE BOOKS

ISBN: 978 1 78037 361 4

First published 2014 by
Bloodaxe Books Ltd,
Eastburn,
South Park,
Hexham,
Northumberland NE46 1BS.

www.bloodaxebooks.com
For further information about Bloodaxe titles
please visit our website or write to
the above address for a catalogue.

Cover design: Neil Astley & Pamela Robertson-Pearce.

Digital reprint of the 2016 Bloodaxe Books second edition.

CONTENTS

INTRODUCTION

Take care whom you mix with in life, irresponsible one,
For if you mix with the wrong people
– And you yourself may be one of the wrong people –
If you make love to the wrong person [...]

They will do you ferocious, indelible harm!
Far beyond anything you can imagine, jazzy sneering one,
And afterwards you'll live in no man's land,
You'll lose your identity, and never get yourself back [...][1]

The disappearance of the poet Rosemary Tonks in the 1970s was
one of the literary world's most tantalising mysteries. For many
years bizarre theories abounded as to her whereabouts – *if* she was
still alive – many of these finding their way into reputable guides.
As Brian Patten put it in a BBC Radio 4 feature in 2009 called
The Poet Who Vanished: 'Rosemary Tonks evaporated into air like
the Cheshire cat.'[2] Nobody seemed to know what had happened to
her and why, the general belief being that she'd found religion, shut
herself away and become a recluse. All her books were out of print
and she was said to have disowned everything she had written.

Having tried to visit her myself, ten years ago, I was aware that
her actual situation was rather different from what everyone had
imagined. But out of respect for her declared wish, maintained by
her family, that she should be left in peace, I told no one what I
knew, continuing to nurse the hope that with encouragement she
might one day relent and allow her poetry to be republished.

Since her death in April 2014 – at the age of 85 – a very dif-
ferent picture has emerged of her later life, shedding new light on
why it was that she turned her back on literature – following a series
of personal tragedies and medical crises – embarking on a self-
torturing spiritual quest which required her to repudiate her own
books. That involved a complete change of identity, from Rosemary
Tonks, the fêted London writer, to the socially challenged Christian

convert Mrs Rosemary Lightband, who lived a mostly solitary life (although not as a recluse) in the seaside town of Bournemouth for the next 35 years.

Over an eleven-year period, from 1963 to 1974, Rosemary Tonks published two epoch-defining poetry collections, *Notes on Cafés and Bedrooms* (1963) and *Iliad of Broken Sentences* (1967),[3] six acerbic, satirical novels,[4] and a number of short stories. She wrote trenchant reviews for leading journals and newspapers, and also collaborated with Hampstead Festival (1965) and the BBC Radiophonic Workshop (1966) on a poetry and sound experimental piece, *Sono-Montage*.[5]

Interviewed in 1967, she declared her direct literary forebears to be Baudelaire and Rimbaud: 'They were both poets of the modern metropolis as we know it and no one has bothered to learn what there is to be learned from them... The main duty of the poet is to excite – to send the senses reeling.'[6]

In sharp contrast with the traditional, well-behaved, dry, self-deprecating verse being published at that time by most of her English contemporaries, her poetry was declamatory, bold, spirited, extravagant and exuberantly sensuous, a hymn to sixties hedonism set amid the bohemian nighttime world of a London reinvented through French poetic influences and sultry Oriental imagery, with the Eliot of *The Waste Land* and 'Prufrock' a ghost in the fog.

Anthony Rudolf praised the 'visionary quality' of her poems: 'They seem to me to have by-passed the Movement poetry of the 1950s and to have emerged from the 1940s poetic matrix of Nicholas Moore, George Barker and J.F. Hendry, poets she would have read in her early twenties. It is a hyper-urban angst-ridden poetry, with ancestry stretching back to Baudelaire's *Spleen de Paris* and the Francophile English symbolists.'[7]

In another interview (see p.116), Tonks asserted:

> I don't understand why poets are quite ready to pick up trivialities, but are terrified of writing of passions. [...] People are born, they procreate, they suffer, they are nasty to one another, they are greedy, they are terribly happy, they have changes in their fortune, and they meet other people who have effects on them, and then they die; and

these thousands of dramatic things happen to them, and they happen to everybody. Everybody has to make terrible decisions or pass examinations, or fall in love, or else avoid falling in love. All these things happen and contemporary poets don't write about them. Why not?[8]

Among the noted admirers of her work in the London literary set were Cyril Connolly ('Miss Tonks's hard-faceted yet musical poems have unexpected power') and A. Alvarez ('real talent of an edgy, bristling kind'). But other critics in the predominantly male poetry world were angered, intimidated or baffled by her poems. For Julian Symons, *Notes on Cafés and Bedrooms* was 'a very odd book, a jumble of images jittered out from Miss Tonks's sub- or semi-consciousness. Many of them are unintelligible to me [...] some are ridiculous, some impressive. [...] The substance of the poems, so far as I understood them, seemed to me pretty thin.'[9]

The negative reviews may have affected her willingness to publish or even to write. 'I have never met anyone who was so hurt by critics,' wrote Terry Coleman in a *Guardian* profile,[10] asking her why this was when poetry critics were 'a second-rate bunch': 'She says she does not want to be killed, all the same.' Inscribing a copy of *Iliad of Broken Sentences* for a friend, she wrote: 'Please forgive me for not writing. Last year I had melancholia. They just smash and smash my poetry. So these are the last roses I shall write.'[11]

Despite being unavailable for four decades, her poetry came to be admired by a new generation – or rather, generations – of poets, from Andrew Motion, Jo Shapcott and Matthew Sweeney to Matthew Caley and John Stammers, who borrowed the title of his collection, *Stolen Love Behaviour* (2005), from her poem 'Badly-chosen Lover' (p.89). I had been excited by her work since first coming across a few of her poems in anthologies. It seemed extraordinary that this amazing poet's work was no longer available, and I followed up various leads over many years in an attempt to trace her, hoping that this new interest from a later generation of readers and writers might persuade her to allow her books to be reissued.

Another longtime advocate, the Berlin-based poet John Hartley Williams (who also died in 2014) wrote a full-length reappraisal of her work for *Poetry Review* in 1996:[12]

> Poets, of course, as we all know, are either of their time or for all time. Rosemary Tonks was both. She wasn't just a poet of the sixties – she was a true poet of any era – but she has sent us strange messages from them, alive, fresh and surprising today... there is possibly no other poet who has caught with such haughty, self-ironising contempt, the loucheness of the period, or the anger it could touch off in brooding bystanders... Rosemary Tonks' imagery has a daring for which it's hard to find a parallel in British poetry.

New York critic John Thompson wrote that 'she produces that unusual thing, a collection of poems that presents a genuine personality, even a character, and a whole way of life'.[13] Yet this was a world which both attracted and repelled her, and she was to turn against its materialism, false values, betrayals and indulgence: 'The mistakes, the wrong people, the half-baked ideas, / And their beastly comments on everything. Foul. / But irresistibly amusing, that is the whole trouble' ('The Little Cardboard Suitcase', p.90).

She was 'Bedouin of the London evening' in one poem (p.69): 'I have been young too long, and in a dressing-gown / My private modern life has gone to waste.'

And 'waste' was how indeed she came to see her life in 'that frightful epoch' – while her own work was 'dangerous rubbish' – when she followed her forebear Rimbaud in renouncing literature totally, believing that Proust, Chekhov, Tolstoy and French 19th-century poetry had carried away her mind, locked her up in libraries, and led her away from ordinary, everyday things, from truth and from God.[14]

Rosemary Tonks was born in 1928 in Gillingham, Kent, the only daughter of Gwendoline (*née* Verdi)[15] and Desmond Tonks, a mechanical engineer who died from Blackwater fever in Nigeria before her birth. His widow gave her the name Rosemary – for remembrance – along with his forenames, christening her Rosemary

Desmond Boswell Tonks. (She was later to use the pseudonym Desmond Tonks when publishing her early poetry: 'Ace of Hooligans' and 'Boy in the Lane' first appeared under that name in Miron Grindea's *Adam international review* in 1956.)[16]

Desmond was the nephew of the surgeon and painter Henry Tonks, who joined the army's medical corps during the First World War and helped Harold Gillies's pioneering work in plastic surgery with his pastels and drawings of facial injury patients. Desmond's brother Myles was married to Gwen's sister Dorothy, who was later to provide Rosemary with refuge in Bournemouth when her life crisis had become unbearable alone.

When her mother was unable to cope, Rosemary had to be looked after in children's homes.[17] They moved house 14 times during the war ('to avoid bombs and people'),[18] and Rosemary was sent at an early age to boarding school at Wentworth College in Bournemouth, which 'turned out each year thirty of the gentlest wives in England'.[19] Precociously brilliant but disruptive and intolerant of authority, she left school at 16. According to accounts[20] questioned by her family, she was expelled. 'I ruined my schooldays through my inability to control myself,' she later recalled.[21]

She was affected by eyesight problems as an infant, with a squint, a lazy left eye and astigmatism in both eyes, which must have reinforced her sense of being separate from others at school and later. Her one constant became literature and her own writing.

By 1946 she was living in Lagos with her mother and new stepfather, 'with a large house, a shotgun, six or seven servants, and attacks of dysentery and malaria'.[22] Like her father, her stepfather was to die in Nigeria. At 18 she was 'back in London with her mother, very poor, and beginning to read Joyce and Baudelaire',[23] discovering public libraries, and hanging out at the Mandrake Club and the Caves de France in Soho, two bohemian wateringholes then at the centre of London's postwar counterculture that were popular with louche artistic types.

Rosemary Tonks was a writer from childhood. A prodigious reader, she wrote children's stories while still at school, one of which, *Miss Bushman-Caldicott*, was broadcast on BBC radio in 1946 and subsequently included in *Uncle Mac's Children's Hour Story Book*. Her first published book, *On Wooden Wings: The Adventures of Webster, written and illustrated by Rosemary Tonks*, followed from John Murray in 1948.

In 1949, aged 20, she married Michael (Micky) Lightband, an engineer (later a financier) six years her senior. Her occupation on the marriage certificate is given as 'writer'. Identifying with Colette in a later essay (p.132), she wrote: 'She was literary to the core, and her effects were calculated, as it was proper they should be.'

Her husband's work took them to India and Pakistan, where she contracted paratyphoid fever in Calcutta, followed by polio in Karachi (in 1952). Recovering from paralysis in England, she was left with a slightly withered right hand. Such was her determination that she taught herself to write and paint with her left hand, and took to wearing a rakish black glove over the other (shown in the photograph of her from 1957 on p.18). These experiences were to feed her portrayal of the young poet who catches polio in her fifth novel, *The Way Out of Berkeley Square* (1970).

With Micky still in Pakistan, she went to live in Paris alone: 'In illness you want to be alone, and England was full of relations.'[24] Living for a year (1952–53) on the Île St Louis, close to the spirits of Baudelaire and Rimbaud, she was able to immerse herself in Parisian culture and French literature, recalling this period in a short memoir published in *The Times* in 1976 (p.157). One of the few surviving photographs of her (p.17) shows a chicly dressed, slender young woman standing in front of Rodin's Stendhal monument in the Jardin du Luxembourg. On a later visit to Paris – in 1967, the centenary of Baudelaire's death – she went to pay homage to the poet in Montparnasse cemetery, lying down beside his life-size effigy on José de Charmoy's Baudelaire monument to confirm that they were the same height.[25]

Reunited the following year in London, the couple set up home in the fashionable area of Downshire Hill, Hampstead, where Rosemary played at being hostess firstly for Micky's business

Rosemary Tonks with a friend (Mrs Trent), *c*. 1948.

Wedding picture (*from left to right*): bridesmaid cousins Wendy and Jill, pageboy Tim, Michael (Micky) Lightband, Rosemary. Holy Trinity Church, Brompton, London, 21 January 1949.

Rosemary in the Jardin du Luxembourg, Paris, *c.* 1952–53.

Rosemary with her husband Micky and mother Gwen at a family wedding gathering at Sweetmans Hall, Pinner, 20 July 1957.

Rosemary working with Alexander Trocchi on *Sono-Montage* at the Stage Sound Library in Covent Garden, May 1965 (photo Clay Perry).

Rosemary Tonks, London, 1969
(photo: Associated Newspapers/REX)

associates and later for her own entourage when her literary career took off. Living just round the corner from Dame Edith Sitwell – and 'hobnobbing' with her, she told family – Rosemary Tonks was a singular figure in London's artistic circles, a world she portrayed with both relish and distaste in sharply observed, semi-autobiographical novels like *The Bloater* (1968), 'the story of a witty, capricious but vulnerable young woman of London, caught in the more than half-serious dilemma of whom to choose as a lover'.[26] Like her alter ego Min in *The Bloater* ('married, but like a reckless little schoolgirl still unbroken'), she was playful, alluring, vivacious and commanded attention. Her cousin Tim Butchard recalls lively evenings in the Hampstead house: 'She effervesced and often held a dinner table spellbound (I remember one with Paul Huxley, Sir Julian Huxley and wife Juliette, Andrew Barrow others)';[27] 'I was mesmerised by her [...] Above all she was terribly, terribly funny, and there was a lot of laughter.'[28]

She also greatly enjoyed the company and conversation of Elias Canetti, fellow habitué of Hampstead's Vienna-style coffee house, the Coffee Cup, where she was photographed by Jane Bown for an *Observer Magazine* feature on 'Poets and Their Worlds' in August 1966 (this book's cover picture is from that shoot). Other friends included the anthropologist Julian Huxley ('I was also investigating similar things, so we got on'),[29] and the fashion designer Thea Porter, who shared her interest in the Tarot.[30]

One of very few other published women poets of that time, she wasn't, however, noted for supporting the sixties sisterhood, being taken to task by Jane Gapen in the *New York Review of Books* for an unsympathetic review (p.122) of Adrienne Rich's *Diving into the Wreck*, which 'should be reviewed from a feminist outlook... It really hurts that a woman would say this about another poet.'[31]

Nor did she feel connected with other poets. 'They are a rather lost set, you know, in London,' she told Peter Orr in 1963. 'They form movements.' (p.116) However, she did form close relationships with both Robert Conquest, the Movement's anthologist, and poet and novelist John Wain. Philip Larkin admired her work, and corresponded with her[32] when editing his *Oxford Book of Twentieth-Century English Verse* (1973), resisting her suggestion that her poem 'Love Territory' (p.45) would represent her better than one of his eventual choices, 'Story of a Hotel Room' (p.68) and 'Farewell to Kurdistan' (p.103).

Geoffrey Godbert recalls meeting her at gatherings of the Group at Edward Lucie-Smith's Chelsea house in the 1970s: 'She immediately gave the impression of a coiled spring waiting and needing to be unsprung. Surrounded by the voices of conventional wisdom, she manifested the loner's stare into, and the need to speak of, the indescribable future before it was too late.'[33]

Anthony Rudolf met her a few times in the mid sixties at the house of their onetime patron, Miron Grindea: 'She was a forceful personality and I recall an argument we had in the presence of Pablo Neruda in Grindea's legendary salon. Her poems matched the forceful personality, being rhetorically explosive, with more exclamation marks than anyone else used.'[34] John Horder also recalls how she 'spoke with an intensity bordering on active aggression'.[35] A Pendennis column in *The Times* in 1965 refers to 'the volatile young poetess Rosemary Tonks'.[36]

Re-reading her work, and talking and corresponding with family and others who knew her, traits soon become apparent which connect the outspoken and uncompromising writer who had no truck with politics (in the novels) or feminism, and was dismissive of any poet whose work she felt lacked integrity or authenticity, with the single-minded born-again Christian convert, the later Mrs Lightband. Despite the divorce she never wanted and could never forgive him for, she kept her ex-husband's name – needed for the new identity – and cut off anyone else in her family who divorced, regardless of fault, including one cousin who had always been dear to her.

The poems are full of damning judgements, insults, extremes, resentments, betrayals and irreconcilable opposites. She writes of her 'intolerance', of being 'powerful, disobedient', and of leading her 'double life among the bores and vegetables'. In 'Diary of a

Rebel' (p.50), she needs the café for her 'fierce hot-blooded sulk-iness'; in 'Poet as Gambler' (p.73), 'gutter and heavens' were her lottery in a 'wasted youth'; in 'Running Away' (p.46) she tears up 'the green rags of the Bible': 'I left the house, I fled / My mother's brow where I had no ambition / But to stroke the writing / I raked in. / [...] I was a guest at my own youth; under / The lamp tossed by a moth for thirteen winters.'

The younger Rosemary comes across as headstrong, wilful, stubborn, obsessive, rebellious, judgemental, fiercely intelligent, and given to extreme ways of thinking. Growing up a widow's only child during the 1930s, packed off to boarding school before and during the war, she was disconnected from other people: 'For this is not my life / But theirs, that I am living. / And I wolf, bolt, gulp it down, day after day' ('Addiction to an Old Mattress', p.97). Much of her fiction also shows a similar sense of disconnection, with other characters perceived as separate from a witty narrator or protagonist, or even observed from some distance as in the short story 'The Pick-up or L'Ercole d'Oro' (p.140). Looking back in her 80s, trying to make sense of her upbringing, she noted: 'No sense of self'.[37]

The last review she published was a long essay on Colette in the *New York Review of Books* (p.132), parts of which read uncannily like versions of her own plight (except that both parties in her own marriage had apparently been unfaithful):

> [Colette's] childish idea of herself had run on unchecked after marriage, and Willy had fostered it; in fact it was *all she had*. Suddenly she found out that he was unfaithful. The shock to her ego was more than it could bear; there was nothing inside capable of withstanding the blow, her personality was fragmented, and she collapsed into a nervous breakdown. At that moment she lost her childhood, and no longer knew who she was. [...] When it was all over, and as soon as she began to write the first *Claudine*, she found herself, and could repair her identity. But this time a new self was in charge. It prescribed physical exercises for her body, and undertook the task of learning how to think, and *be*; the spirit stopped still and listened – an Oriental skill.

During her childhood, her widowed mother had sought guidance from mediums, and Rosemary thought her mother's life and her own had been harmed by their self-fulfilling prophecies as well as by the church. Like her mother, she was superstitious, but took this to an extreme, believing in signs and omens that showed the presence of evil spirits. There was cause and effect in supernatural occurrences, and she came to see almost everything in life as black or white, good or evil.

The sudden death of her mother Gwen in a freak accident in the spring of 1968 precipitated a personal crisis. Believing the church had failed her ailing mother when she'd most needed its help, Rosemary turned her back on Christianity, and for the next eight years attended spiritualist meetings, consulted mediums and healers, and took instruction from Sufi "seekers". She cites several examples of these in a letter to Thea Porter:

> Mir Bashir the palmist is really v. good – but so brusque in manner that it makes you angry. I had a curious session with a healer called David Hadda last night, his hands have the same effect as volcanic mud – make your own roasting hot & tingling. However I had to erase my personality and make an exit, because a certain amount of psychological bullying goes with the healing, and I can't bear any form of attempted subjugation.[38]

The inspiring presence in her house of a collection of ancient artefacts, including Oriental god figures, led to her approaching a Chinese spiritual teacher and an American yoga guru. All these she repudiated in turn.

Following the collapse of her marriage, she entered the solitary later phase of her life. By 1977 she was living just a few doors away from her ex-husband (soon to be joined by a new wife) on Downshire Hill, doing Taoist meditation, writing reviews and working on a new novel. But other misfortunes followed: a burglary in which she lost all her clothes; a law-suit costing thousands of pounds; and ill-health, including incapacitating neuritis in her one good arm.

Rosemary attributed her next life disaster to her difficult Taoist eye exercises, which involved staring for hours at a blank wall, turning the eyes in and looking intensely at bright objects. On the last day of December 1977, she was admitted to Middlesex Hospital for emergency operations on detached retinas in both eyes, which saved her eyesight but left her nearly blind for the next few years. This was her reward for 'ten long years searching for God'. Unable to see properly, emaciated and 'psychologically smashed', she couldn't cook or shop, and rarely left home. Following a whole series of personal crises, this isolating experience of near-blindness which continued with only minimal improvements over many months must have been traumatic, with the sensory deprivation involved possibly helping to trigger a gradual shift in her mental state.[39]

She had been discussing – since November 1976 – the publication of a selection of her poems by John Moat and John Fairfax's Phoenix Press in Newbury. This was to include 34 of the poems from her two collections from Putnam and Bodley Head, both publishers having first declined to release paperback editions after the hardbacks had sold out, before stopping publishing poetry altogether: 'Which is the reason I am landed as I am,' she wrote to John Moat.[40] In August 1977, she commented:

> Some of these poems will need revision. I know what's wrong; it will take a few days.
>
> The poems go into 4 categories. Travel, the Life, Love, Early Youth. I'll come up with a special title for the book. Titles are most important. If I do finish the novel on time, then I will indeed compose a new poem – it used to take me up to 2 months. (Long ones 3 months) I have a bundle of notes sitting here waiting, but then so does the bill for rates, and although I am financially OK at the moment I'm concerned to be able to maintain my way of life into the future and until death. No one's going to pay me for writing poems![41]

But there were to be no more poems (or revisions). By July 1978 she was still struggling to recover from her ordeal:

> I've had the most tremendous fight, month after month alone, to get back sight to what it was before op. I shall make it, with God's help. Am doing it – or rather He is. The thing is that I am worn down & so weak & wasted by the struggle

25

that everything is the most terrible effort. And it has to go on – as this thing takes months to heal, a friend tells me. [...] I cannot work on the poems at moment, I can just about write this letter. [...]

You could publish them as they are, uncorrected by me. But they will have no support (from novel & other books in preparation) & will sink like a stone & be lost all over again. By the autumn/winter I should be able to get the novel to my agent.[42]

Her struggles continued. Writing a year later:

The thing is that I am still fighting for my eyes. At last something is happening. I am keeping a record: it is incredible. Everything is agony, you see. Last year just having them open was agony – & couldn't see when they were. Now it seems a door might have opened for me: I am getting discharge from both eyes, and a hundred other things. I am being healed. [...]

I plan to spend the winter at my aunt's, very slowly correcting my big book.[43]

Later that autumn she left London for Bournemouth, given refuge at her aunt Dorothy's flat, where again she looked for help from spiritualists – this time Charismatics and Pentecostalists – before coming to the realisation that her own spiritual truth lay only in the Bible itself, especially the New Testament, the first book she was able to read as her sight began slowly to return, albeit imperfectly.

Deciding to settle in Bournemouth, she tried for several months during 1980 to sell her London house, but each time a buyer turned up the sky would darken and there would be a foul smell in the house. This happened so often that she ruled out coincidence. She cleaned every room obsessively and threw out all her books on spiritualism and the occult, all to no avail. Finally, believing that the Oriental religious artefacts that filled the house must be exerting some malign power, she packed them all into five suitcases and got help to have them deposited in the vault of Barclays Bank in Hampstead. She saw these as sinister objects, stolen from temples and graves, which had led her to seek knowledge of God through what she now believed to be a diabolical Eastern religion. The very next day a young couple came to see the house in bright sunshine, loved it and bought it.

In November 1980 she moved into Old Forest Lodge, a mostly hidden house tucked away behind the sea-front, where she was known to neighbours as Mrs Lightband. Here she was to cut herself off totally from her former life, eventually refusing to see or to respond to letters from relatives, old friends, or publishers like myself whose hopes had to be dashed. It wasn't an easy place for anyone to find, with no nameplate or number on the door; the curtains were kept closed to deter would-be visitors, and knocks on the door and rings on the doorbell were rarely answered.

There she resolved to free herself of all the remaining kinds of 'bondage'. She had broken with her last healer, who had failed to cure her eyesight problems, having realised she'd become psychologically dependent upon him. To escape the pull of other healers, mediums, spiritualists and evil spirits, she turned to the Bible, which became her 'complete manual' for living. Next to go were sleeping tablets, which she'd been on for most of her life; shaving a little more off each tablet with a razor each day, she managed to wean herself off them totally after a year. Once totally free, she would be baptised.

Still troubled by what she took to be supernatural occurrences, she felt she must still be in bondage to other forces, and embarked on an act which was later to sadden her family when they learned of it after her death. She decided to destroy her collection of Oriental treasures – a bequest from an aunt by marriage – which were 'graven images' that had to be burned by fire, according to the Second Commandment. Retrieving the five suitcases by taxi and train from London, she filled two garden incinerators with over 40 artefacts itemised in a handwritten list titled 'The burning of some idols (11 August 1981)', and set fire to them. These included three Tang horses with riders, four Sung priest figures, a Japanese warrior, a Korean dancing figure, Chinese jade and small bronzes,

Chinese silk robes embroidered with dragons, carved Chinese letter seals (rose apricot stone), Chinese dogs on stands, chess-set and lion mask, along with other artefacts of marble, terracotta, porcelain, plaster, mother-of-pearl, ivory, wood and stone, from China, Korea, Japan, Africa, Greece, Bali and Persia.

Over the next few days she smashed and hammered at the still intact Tang and Sung figures until she got the remnants down to 'dog-biscuit size'. All this while, she said, there were noises in the house, and a mile and half away, another house was wrecked by flying objects and furniture thrown about by a poltergeist which had to be exorcised. The local Bournemouth newpapers for that week document those other occurrences (she kept the cuttings), which were witnessed not just by the household concerned but by four other people including a policeman.

That left what she called her 'profession' to be confronted. She still had the manuscript of an unpublished novel ('the best thing I had ever written'), about a man's search for God, written during the six years leading up to her eye operation, but a medium had recounted the entire plot to her, complete with detailed descriptions of all the characters, which meant the book must be dangerous and could lead others astray:

> I was afraid I would be pursued for my latest manuscript [100,000 words: first half of a novel the size of 'War & Peace': 6 years worth] I burnt it on the incinerator here in the garden. Well, you don't do all that without excellent reasons! Never mind the fame, I was burning many thousands of pounds. I burnt it, together with all the copies and notes. I can tell you I meant business! [44]

She had already contacted John Moat withdrawing the selection of poems which the Phoenix Press was to have published. The fate of an extended essay on Baudelaire is unknown: this was to have been appeared in the US in 1977, probably in the *New York Review of Books*, where she had earlier published two other articles. Responding to a query from her great-niece Lucy Reynolds in a later letter, she wrote:

> No: I don't write poetry now.

I was building up my Academic reputation when my eye op. came along. This meant articles for 'the Times' or The Obs (I remember I actually did a translation of a poem by Botticelli for them! Amazing waste of time.) or the 'New York Review of Books'. It was prestige work for tuppence. But I found the mental training very useful. Now that I study the Bible, this past discipline has been a enormous advantage. Exactly the preparation needed because your mind is alerted to unravelling mysteries hidden in words.[45]

That October she travelled to Jerusalem and was baptised near the River Jordan on 17 October 1981, the day before her 53rd birthday. Obliterating her former identity as the writer Rosemary Tonks, she dated her new life from that 'second birth'. Mostly keeping herself to herself, for the next 34 years she lived an insular, private life, quite comfortable in her circumstances, defiantly independent but isolated in her continuing search for God, always alert to the 'brainwashing', controlling or manipulating tendencies in the religious groups and beliefs she encountered.

Ever restless in spirit, she fought daily battles with her inner demons, plagued by self-doubt and frequent bouts of debilitating depression which could only be lifted by asserting her absolute belief in God's love for her. In this she was helped by the ways in which her magical thinking had developed over the course of her later solitary life: birds were her soundscape, and birds were associated with her mother, whom she called 'Birdie'; and she would interpret soft calls or harsh caws or cries from crows and seagulls in particular as comforting messages or warnings from the Lord, and would base decisions on what to do, whom to trust, whether to go out, how to deal with a problem, on how these bird sounds made her feel. Depression was Satan trying to weaken her, but a positive feeling from God would drive him out and restore her well-being. She also only had to hear particular pieces of music on the radio and what she called 'the Flood' would immediately be lifted from her: Rimsky-Korsakov's 'Scheherazade', Borodin's 2nd String Quartet ('a message of exquisite sound from the Lord stilling & resting the whole body with the heart's joy'), and Bach's

'Jesus Joy of Man's Desiring'.[46] All these were pieces her mother had loved and played to her in her childhood. And of course Scheherazade saves her life every day by telling stories.

Clearly, Rosemary suffered in her later life from what some would categorise as a "borderline personality disorder". She avoided talking to other people wherever possible, regarding them as 'slaves of Satan', keeping any verbal or physical contact (including necessary communication with people in shops and on buses) to the absolute minimum, sometimes handing people notes because talking personally with almost anyone could push her into one of her black depressive states, as would any kind of stress or emotional upset. Sadly, she blocked attempts by concerned family members to offer help or to stay in touch with her, finding any such contact so emotionally overwhelming that she became terrified even of speaking a few words on the telephone, knowing this would set off another attack of 'the Flood'.

But she adapted her life to this condition, managing practical arrangements in appropriate ways, and analysing everything that happened to her with intelligence and articulacy in the notebooks she kept, right through to her mid 80s, using these as a kind of self-therapy. Believing totally in the efficacy of what most other people would see only as signs or omens, she interpreted symbols and metaphors in literal, Manichean ways. Her bouts of depression were caused by Satan and her thoughts at such times were not hers but ones he was putting into her head. She was married to the Lord and therefore couldn't feel lonely; when she did so, or had other doubts or anxieties, this was Satan undermining her.

I'm not qualified to attempt a psychological reading of her condition, which seems to have evolved and become more complex over many years, but discussions I have had with three psycho-therapists[47] suggest that it must have been rooted in childhood separation and rejection trauma, and in never having had any sense of a strong, secure attachment to other people from birth, exacerbated by her mother's death, her feelings of betrayal and rejection, her near blindness with prolonged sensory deprivation and isolation, and the other personal crises. Depression is often associated with rage which cannot be expressed, and having only one fragile parent – with her dead father experienced as an absence she could never fill herself – would have made anger unsafe for an insecure only child. Anger is internalised, directed more inside the self, and the more that anger grows, the more frightening it becomes; and so is configured as a Satan or self-damaging voice inside as a way of containing it, as an inner world response to trauma.

Rosemary Tonks's own analysis of Colette's personal crisis is apposite here: 'The shock to her ego was more than it could bear; there was nothing inside capable of withstanding the blow, her personality was fragmented, and she collapsed into a nervous breakdown' (p.136). This reads almost like a textbook description of trauma, very like the one which Freud gives in *Beyond the Pleasure Principle*: when our 'protective shield' is shattered, it leads to fragmentation.[47]

Her belief in God served as another kind of protective shield. Everything could be explained and made safe with the Lord protecting her from Satan. Unfortunately, her extraordinary literary talent was the great casualty in this scheme. 'I couldn't read a book now, it wouldn't have meaning for me,' she noted in 1999:

> What are books? They are minds, Satan's minds.
> How foolish they are!! When you think of the Lord![48]

> Devils gain access through the mind: printed books carry, each one, an evil mind: which enters your mind.[49]

But all this takes nothing away from the brilliance and originality of the regrettably small body of poetry she wrote as Rosemary Tonks in her 20s and 30s, before she was overwhelmed by events and changes in her life (and in her being) outside her control.

After undergoing what was by design and effect a complete change in her identity, Rosemary Lightband, as she became, rejected not just her own books, but *all* books apart from the Bible (the Koran along with sacred texts from other faiths all served false gods and were anathema to her).

When Rosemary Lightband visited libraries – which remained favourite haunts, along with cafés – it was to read Scripture, preferably from the Tyndale Bible, the first English translation, if they had it, or if not then from later King James Bible which drew on Tyndale. More modern Bibles were travesties of the Word. Yet she never stopped questioning the nature of the self, as she wrote to Lucy Reynolds:

> Yes, I do so agree that we should treat the human brain with respect. Here's an interesting thing you discover: you are where your mind is. The other day I was in an old junk shop here, talking to the owner – and suddenly I looked around for Ga! Reason: the last time – say 5 years before – I had been with that person, among those objects, she had been with me. I had just slipped back 5 years, and was 100% back there. So the mind [spirit] is outside time. Proust discovered the same thing: but he never followed up the huge implications. Only the body is within time, and subject to eventual destruction. But the mind is a spiritual thing, a spiritual 'body'. Since people can't see a spirit, they don't take the matter seriously. But you can see a spirit expressing itself in someone's body – there it is, activating the whole body. And you know at once what kind of a spirit it is, nice or nasty. Of course, we also have non-human spirits [minds] going about invisibly on the world; the evidence being those awful temples containing horrible effigies, all over the East.[50]

Contrary to what everyone who had known her believed, Rosemary was not a recluse. During the early 1980s she 'began to search for a church bicycling across England'. And just as in her London years, she continued to inhabit cafés and parks, and was active as a silent, often solitary evangelist working outside any church, giving out Bibles around Bournemouth and in London. Ordering Bibles in different languages from the Trinitarian Bible Society, she made numerous trips on Saturdays or Sundays to Speakers' Corner in London to give these to potential converts, from the mid 1990s until August 2012, by which time the travel and effort involved had become too much for her.

Every summer she reviewed the investment income she lived off, and made sure she had donated exactly ten per cent of her earnings from the previous tax year to charities. On 30 May 2012, she noted: 'Spent all day doing sums re my Income & my tithing: I love tithing, it makes me happy. Then ran down to Barclays in the sunshine, & got in just in time. Bank closes at 5pm.'[51]

She mellowed in her more peaceful later years, and is said to have been popular with staff at the Piccadilly Hotel just round the corner from her house, where she went to have Christmas dinner every year on her own. She even made one friend there, who remembers her as kind, happy and always laughing. In April 2012 she decided she 'must do something about being so cut off from people',[52] and started attending Open Air Mission meetings in Bournemouth on Saturdays, even having tea in cafés with some of the Christians she met there and rather reluctantly attending a few of their church services.

Finally, in November 2012, she wrote to the cousin she had cut off years earlier to apologise: 'I was boxed up, under the most frightful, frightful mental pressure. I was not myself. All my decisions were wrong, inhuman, appalling. Give me time, please, I long to explain it to you.'[53] But no such opportunity was to arise.

In February 2013 she spent several days in hospital, moving into temporary accommodation in the Piccadilly Hotel on being discharged, from where she wrote two further letters to the cousin, but only about her difficulties and immediate plans. Her failing health had made it impossible for her to continue to live alone at Old Forest Lodge, which she sold in May 2013, downsizing to a serviced garden flat not far from her old house after selling, giving away or destroying most of her possessions.

She had only been there for four months when she was again taken to hospital by ambulance, having collapsed with exhaustion, caused by ovarian cancer. After three weeks of treatment, she was taken to a nursing home: 'Horrors!! All the residents either demented or on the way to it. Staff very nice. Was absolutely terrified & lost. Decided I must leave at once. That very day. They wanted me to stay overnight. No. Must leave at once. [...] called a taxi & I came post haste back to the flat. Loved it! Slept all night!!'[54]

She spent the last three months of 2013 back in her flat, but much of January 2014 in hospital, and then only had a few more weeks at home before she had to be taken to a different nursing home. She died on 15 April 2014 and was buried two weeks later in her mother's grave at the Church of St Thomas à Becket, Warblington, Hampshire, without a funeral or any ceremony, in line with her wishes: the body was only a vessel for the spirit. She left instructions that the inscription on her headstone should read: 'Rosemary Desmond Boswell Lightband'.

I first wrote to Mrs Rosemary Lightband in 2004, not knowing that her ex-husband Micky had died that same year. She never responded. After further attempts to make contact, I called on her in Bournemouth in 2006 after writing beforehand. But just as when family members had tried to see her on many occasions, mine was a fruitless visit, although I was able to put them in touch with one of her neighbours, who was good enough to keep them informed about any changes in her situation – which can't have been easy with her running away whenever she was spotted, believing that this kind man was another one of Satan's slaves.

Three years later, hoping she might relent and allow her poetry to be republished after hearing of the new interest in her work from a new generation – or generations – of poets and readers, I sent her a couple of postcards to let her know about the radio programme, *The Poet Who Vanished*, picturing her sitting on her own, listening to several of today's poets sharing their enthusiasm for her poetry as if this lost writer were another person. Would she reconnect with her past self?

I know now that this lost writer was indeed another person as far as she was concerned. She wrote down the broadcast dates in her diary, along with a note: 'second postcard from Satan'. The day the programme went out she wasn't even at home in Bournemouth, but was sitting on a deckchair at Speakers' Corner in London, giving away Bibles in different languages, still trying to win converts to the faith.

The list of treasures recorded in 'The burning of the idols' could have graced a Sothebys catalogue. This was a collection of works created by devout artists from other faiths assembled by a knowledgeable collector who loved the art of ancient China and other cultures, all given to Rosemary Tonks on trust. Reading through this account, line by line, felt like the antithesis of Edmund de Waal's redeeming tale *The Hare with the Amber Eyes*, in which a family history is brought to life through the netsuke figures passed on from one generation to the next through times of war, devastation and great personal loss.

The treasures passed on to Rosemary Tonks from her aunt are lost forever. The one great gift she has left us – her books of poetry – used to survive only in the libraries of collectors. Commenting on this situation in the aftermath of her death, Oliver Kamm wrote in *The Times*:

> Her art, she had decided, was dangerous rubbish. The Bible was what mattered. She burnt the manuscript of her last novel and instructed publishers to remove her poems from anthologies.
>
> I find this a deeply saddening mental state and, if the decision were mine, I'd have no hesitation in giving permission for Tonks's work to be published now. The creator of a work of art can no more decide its fate than he or she can decide its critical reputation. [...] In death, Rosemary Tonks deserves the respect of rediscovery.[55]

I know I must share the delight of many thousands of readers that Rosemary Tonks's family – not without much hesitation and careful consideration – decided in the end to agree with that sentiment. There was no ban on republication in her will, written many years after she ceased to be Rosemary Tonks, so that her books didn't even exist for her then. The woman who destroyed that priceless collection given to her on trust seems to me a very different person from the author of those marvellously edgy and timeless poems.

NEIL ASTLEY

ACKNOWLEDGEMENTS & NOTES

This book could not have been published – nor this introduction written – without the support and assistance of the Rosemary Tonks Estate, and I wish to thank her cousins Jill Brandt, Wendy Reynolds and Tim Butchard for their kindness and help over a number of years, and most of all, for being open to make a difficult decision to act in the interests of the work for which they became responsible.

In revising the introduction for this second edition, I have been able to refer to letters written by Rosemary Tonks which have come to light since the book was first published, and in particular wish to thank Rosemary's great-niece, Lucy Reynolds, for giving me access to letters she received in 1988-90, as well as Venetia Porter, for access to letters written to her mother, Thea Porter. I must also thank Thea Smith for her work on *Sono-Montage*, and Sarah Robins for the family photograph on page 18.

This introduction includes some material previously included in an obituary (2 May 2014) and an article entitled 'Rosemary Tonks, the lost poet' (31 May 2014) published in *The Guardian*, and I am grateful to the paper for allowing me to draw upon those pieces.

I would also like to thank in particular, for various kinds of help: Peter Armstrong, Sabina ffrench Blake, Denis Brandt, Sue Corbett, Vivien Green, Christine Hall, John Halliday, Clare Lindsay, John Moat, Pamela Robertson-Pearce, Brian Patten, Anthony Rudolf, Thea Smith, Henry Summers, the late John Hartley Williams, and Nicholas Wroe.

This second edition includes an additional prose piece, 'On being down, but not quite out, in Paris', first published in 1976 (see p.157), as well as excerpts from correspondence and expanded footnotes drawing on material which has come to light since the first edition was published in 2014.

1. Rosemary Tonks, 'Done for!', see p.100.
2. 'Rosemary Tonks: The Poet Who Vanished', BBC Radio 4 *Lost Voices* series, first broadcast 29 March 2009, repeated 4 April 2009, presented by Brian Patten, produced by Christine Hall.
3. *Notes on Cafés and Bedrooms* (Putnam, 1963); *Iliad of Broken Sentences* (The Bodley Head, 1967).
4. *Emir* (Adam Books, 1963); *Opium Fogs* (Putnam, 1963); *The Bloater* (1968), *Businessmen as Lovers* (1969) [published in the US as *Love Among the Operators*], *The Way Out of Berkeley Square* (1970) and *The Halt During the Chase* (1972), all from The Bodley Head.
5. The first version of *Sono-Montage* was performed at Hampstead Festival in May 1965 by Rosemary Tonks and four other poets including Alexander Trocchi with an experimental sound track devised with Lorna Coates of the Stage Sound Library in Covent Garden. Billed as 'an experiment in combining spoken poetry with electronically produced sounds', the radio version was recorded in November 1965, produced by George MacBeth and first broadcast on the BBC's Third Programme on 21 June 1966, with an introduction by

Rosemary Tonks (the purpose of using electronics was 'to put a dramatic edge on poems read aloud') followed by her own readings of 'Poet as Gambler', 'Badly-chosen Lover' and 'Orpheus in Soho', interwoven with two poems each read by Michael Baldwin, Peter Redgrove and Paul Roche, counterpointed with a sound track adapted by Delia Derbyshire and the BBC's Radiophonic Workshop in Maida Vale. Tonks later drew upon these experiences for her novel *The Bloater* (1968), whose central protagonist Min works in a sound studio. For a full account of the making of *Sono-Montage*, see Thea Smith's thesis 'Rosemary Tonks: Sculpting Sound and Poetry in Sono-Montage' (*Archaeologies of Criticism*, Royal College of Art, April 2015).

Rosemary Tonks's contributions to *Sono-Montage* were heard again for the first time in fifty years as part of an event curated by Lucy Reynolds at Flat Time House, Peckham, on 31 January 2015; and again at an event presented by me with Lucy Reynolds at Ledbury Poetry Festival on 11 July 2015.

6. Diary article by John Horder, *The Times*, 16 October 1967.

7. Anthony Rudolf, email, 8 May 2014.

8. Interview with Peter Orr, 22 July 1963. See p.115.

9. Julian Symons, 'Smartening Up', *The Spectator*, 9 May 1963.

10. Terry Coleman, 'Rosemary for remembrance: Terry Coleman talks to Rosemary Tonks', *The Guardian*, 24 October 1970.

11. Philip Annis, email, 30 March 2009. This was an inscribed (undated) copy he had bought from a second-hand bookseller.

12. John Hartley Williams, 'Downhill, Mad as Swine', *Poetry Review*, 11 no.4 (Winter 1996).

13. John Thompson, 'An Alphabet of Poets', *New York Review of Books*, 11 no.2, 1 August 1968.

14. This paragraph and subsequent unsourced summaries draw upon 'Surgery on Both Eyes and Conversion', a private holograph document written by Rosemary Lightband in 1990 for her cousins, which they allowed me to read to help me give an accurate, balanced account of her life in the obituary and feature published in *The Guardian*. Since it was not intended for publication, I have paraphrased its content, only including direct quotation in a few instances where it was important that a particular word or phrase of hers be used.

15. Rosemary Tonks said this of her Verdi ancestry (which may be fanciful) writing to John Moat: 'I'm bound to have strong ideas, I always do, and I hope we won't rub too much against the good friendship. My grandfather's uncle, Giuseppe Verdi, was born on the 10th of a certain powerful month, and I was born on the 17th of that same month. He had to have his own way, in order to transform Italian opera, and I inherit one or two physical features – and other hidden stubborn traits, connected with having my own way. My grandfather himself was a Prince of the Rosy Cross, a great spiritual power, whom we shall be happy is on our side. So we are set fair for this book!' Letter to John Moat, 30 August 1977. University of Exeter, Special Collections Archives (GB 0029) EUL MS 230/4, Literary and personal papers of John Moat (hereinafter University of Exeter).

16. Adam international review, 257 (1956).

17. Rosemary Lightband, notebook 129 (16 July 2012).

18. Rosemary Lightband, notebook 121 (20 December 2009).

19. Terry Coleman, *ibid.*

20. Including Terry Coleman, *ibid.*

21. Rosemary Lightband, notebook 135 (18 October 2013).

22. Terry Coleman, *ibid.*

23. Terry Coleman, *ibid.*

24. Terry Coleman, *ibid.* See also 'On being down, but not quite out, in Paris' (1976) on pages 157-59.

25. Terry Coleman, *ibid.*

26. *The Bloater* (The Bodley Head, 1968), dustjacket note.

27. Tim Butchard, email, 21 August 2014.

28. Tim Butchard, speaking at Ledbury Poetry Festival, 11 July 2015.

29. 'I remember Francis Huxley [old friend from my Hampstead days] somehow "went native" in London. Quite an achievement really! He had wind-bells hanging up in his flat, and took up with spooky-type women, and began to produce spooky books. He was very nice, but Anthropology, ostensibly his subject, somehow got into his bones and carried him away to the never-neverland. At the time I was also investigating similar things, so we got on. But now I see the great dangers of trying to take on board primitive black magic cultures – and imagining you could get away unharmed yourself. The Hindu religion is death, of course. All those carved figures represent demons – and if we Westerners think demons don't exist, any Hindu "priest" [or for that matter Buddhist] will quickly disillusion you! They do all those peculiar things [rituals, meditation, chanting, and all that rubbish] to ward off evil spirits. And nobody gets up to all those ridiculous antics without good reason. When Francis got involved he was playing with fire. I don't think he has surfaced. Look what happened to John Lennon.' Letter to Lucy Reynolds, 15 December 1988.

30. Rosemary Tonks's correspondence (1971-79) with Thea Porter includes much discussion of the Tarot, clairvoyants, healers and sufis. Her daughter Venetia Porter: 'My mother was extremely into Tarot, astrology etc. so that was clearly an immediate bond. Unfortunately for my mother she governed her entire business by it!' (email, 31 December 2014).

31. Jane Gapen, 'Women and Poetry', *New York Review of Books*, 20 no.19, 29 November 1973.

32. Hull University Archives, Papers of Philip Arthur Larkin, correspondence between Rosemary Tonks and Philip Larkin, 6–22 July 1972 (U DPL2/3/61/39).

33. Geoffrey Godbert, Letter, *The Guardian*, 8 June 2014.

34. Anthony Rudolf, *ibid.*

35. John Horder, *ibid.*

36. Pendennis, 'Mixing up noises', *The Observer*, 23 May 1965.

37. Rosemary Lightband, diary note, 20 April 2010.

38. Letter to Thea Porter, 20 July 1971.

39. Peter Armstrong suggested that sensory deprivation during the long period of near blindness and isolation could have been a factor here.

40. Letter to John Moat, 26 November 1976, University of Exeter.

41. Letter to John Moat, 30 August 1977, University of Exeter.

42. Letter to John Moat, 27 July 1978, University of Exeter.

43. Letter to John Moat, 18 September 1979, University of Exeter.

44. Letter to Lucy Reynolds, 15 December 1988. Written in the margin next to this paragraph, she added: 'I didn't like what I had written, and thought it was harmful.'

45. Letter to Lucy Reynolds, 21 December 1987.

46. Rosemary Lightband, notebook 129 (2 June 2012).

47. This introduction owes much to discussions and email exchanges I've had with three psychotherapists, Peter Armstrong, John Halliday and Clare Lindsay. This paragraph and the following one paraphrase comments made by Clare Lindsay.

48. Rosemary Lightband, notebook 85 (23 March 1999).

49. Rosemary Lightband, notebook 85 (27 March 1999).

50. Letter to Lucy Reynolds, 17 December 1990.

51. Rosemary Lightband, notebook 128 (30 May 2012).

52. Rosemary Lightband, notebook 128 (11 April 2012).

53. Letter to Jill Brandt, 28 November 2012.

54. Rosemary Lightband, notebook 135 (21 September 2013).

55. Oliver Kamm, Notebook, *The Times*, 10 June 2014.

Notes on Cafés and Bedrooms

(1963)

This is the first collected volume of a young poet who is also a novelist. Rosemary Tonks is a Londoner, living in Hampstead; she has published two children's books, and reviews poetry for the BBC European Service. 'My ethos,' she writes, 'is a great European Metropolis; I want to show human passions at work and to give eternal forces their contemporary dimension in this landscape.' Her sensuous diction explores a world of metropolitan moods and relationships, presenting an individual and exciting vision.

Recommendation of the Poetry Book Society

Jacket note, *Notes on Cafés and Bedrooms* (Putnam, 1963)

To Micky

Love Territory

To F.U.

He's timid with women, and the dusk is excruciating
The bronze-brown autumn dusk!
And the half-lit territories of street and bed and heart
Are savage and full of risk.

On bronze nights
When the territory is half-lit by casual glances
He sweats, each step is hideous!
Once he knows his strength of course he will be ruthless.

Bedrooms – he'll force an entrance,
On an evening full of leaves and blood and water,
By the elemental half-light of a passing glance.

Oh these brown nights are excruciating!
When the quarter's full of gold air, very cold to breathe,
Lovers embrace at dusk with an enlightened coarseness
That makes the frigid grind their teeth.

In the deep bronze, when he goes out to acquit himself
It's treacherous and elemental
In the half-dark of a street, a bed, a heart.
And also modern, young and gentle.

Running Away

In the green rags of the Bible I tore up
The straight silk of childhood on my head
        I left the house, I fled
My mother's brow where I had no ambition
        But to stroke the writing
           I raked in.

She who dressed in wintersilk my head
That month when there is baize on the high wall
Where the dew cloud presses its lustration,
And the thrush is but a brooch of rain
As the world flies softly in the wool of heaven.

        I was a guest at my own youth; under
The lamp tossed by a moth for thirteen winters
        Sentenced to cabbage and kisses
By She who crammed an Earth against my feet and
        Pulled over me the bright rain
           Storm of fleece.

Not for me – citizenship of the backdoor
Where even the poor wear wings; while on Sunday
Gamy ventilations raise their dilettante
In the bonnet of the satin-green dung fly,
And fungus sweats a livery of epaulettes.

I was a hunter whose animal
Is that dark hour when the hemisphere moves
        In deep blue blaze of dews
And you, brunette of the birdmusic tree,
                Stagger in spat diamonds
                        Drunkenly.

Like some Saint whose only blasphemy is a
Magnificent juice vein that plucks his groin
With April's coarse magicianship as green
As the jade squirt of fruit, I was the child whose breast
Rocks to a muscle savage as Africa.

        Thundercloud, your wool was rough with mud
As the coat of a wild beast on which flowers grow,
                Your brogue of grunts so low
        They left soil in the mouth. After you, I
                Walked as through a Djinn's brain
                        Gleaming lane.

I was incriminated by your hammer
In my chest. And forfeit to the crepe hoods
Of my mother's eyes; the iron door of her oven
And her church. Skies, cut to blind, had but laid on
Her priest's mouth the green scabs of winter.

                But I had the marvellous infection!
                Leaning upon my fairy and my dog
                        In the ultramarine
        Latitudes of dew shook like a tear that's carried
                Through darkness on the knuckles of
                        A woman's glove.

I saw each winter where my hen-thrush
Left her fork in famine's white banqueting cloth;
Could I not read as well the tradesman's hand
With its magenta creases – whose soul turns blandly
On a sirloin mattress to smile at the next meal?

O She who would paper her lamp with my wings!
That hour when all the Earth is drinking the
                    Blue drop of thunder; and in
Dark debris as of a magician's room, my beast
                    A scented breathing
                              To the East.

20th Century Invalid

I am sick mortar and anonymous
Like that night worker
Who must wreck his health
By eating fog in cities
Laid up very still in breath.
But do not blame my illness
On the grave that digs itself
From 'one day' to my shoe
And nudges to be stuffed.

The fault lies with the tutor
Who gave too powerful an instruction
In Creation, that I am stricken
And anonymous on city nights,
Who had no right to show me Earth
Abroad in Limbo with her clouds
That browse about her in bright fleets,
Or deeply with his thumbprint mark
The softly-beating mortar of my heart.

He knew that his tuition
In so powerful a Creation
That roosts abroad in Ether
Thickly hung with blazing fleece,
Would groom me for damnation
In the city among men
For to bite the dust anonymous
At night is twice as bitter
When the appetite is great.

Diary of a Rebel

For my fierce hot-blooded sulkiness
I need the café – where old mats
Of paper lace catch upon coatsleeves
That are brilliant with the nap of idleness

...And the cant of the meat-fly is eternal!
On the window is the milk of lazy breath,
And the coalcart rumbles – with huge purses
Full of dust and narcotics for the masses!

Sin pricks me like a convict's suit of arrows
For here my evil, blue, and moody youth
Has found its old lair... at the bottom
Of the soil path in the bed of stinging nettles

That are splashed with wood milk
And have every hair upon them raised to strike!
There is no trade can lure me out with bundle,
Noose, and feeding-bag; I know that fate

Has graves to fill in daily life,
And the jargon of the meat-fly's leaded wing
To put to sleep the citizen
Employed in keeping worms at bay by breathing.

Bedroom in an Old City

In the room with the water mark as rich
as sago on the wall, the young head of a minx
asleep sheds on cheap linen the pale silk hair
of baby Kensington.

An apricot fabric, hanging in wads lightly
grimed, admits morning. The furnishings have
picked themselves clothing as country bushes
with hooks are able to dress from passing chil-
dren. A tumbler of green beach glass with some
spillings, bright water ovals firm on dust, is
the bedside comfort.

Against hair and sheet the mesmerised face
is very slightly active. Paint burns from yes-
terday's gouache are healing on the mouth; it
passes some great supernatural illness with the
zither of a little healthy breath. The shorthand
typist at seventeen: on either side of warm
nostril she presses crossly to her cheek the
stiff gilt lashes of a court page.

In the underframe of the window, beading
records a lorry from the world; buzz of a
giant 'cello string. A chest of drawers
take the itch of the infection.

Streets have begun.

A lapel dog with goblet eyes of hot
seccotine stamps on brass toes to where a
black tree eats gravel; the snout at the urinal
shiny as the chinpad of a violin. Labourers,
their ringlets scented with blue grease,
assemble at some work of coloured mud. A
tradesman with the specific violence and
well-being of butchers steps out for his
attractive marble shop of quartered bodies;
glazed cheeks of the very best meat, these
have been costly feeders since he was a
young soldier handsome as a tulip and badly
finished at the hands.

In the distance, weather can be seen
thrusting and gleaming. A diamond cutter
has been over the metropolis. The atmosphere
has spat once or twice on fish and magazines.

A sharp piece of blond sugar rattles in
the mouth of a newsboy; he lubricates and
passes with a humid bag of language. Infant
snob, he adjusts precociously his printed
jargon sheets to door and nameplate. With
its ingenious crimes, the civilisation is
comprehensive; it is not necessary to take the
rest of the world seriously. But in order
that they may be said to think deeply, people
go to the trouble of believing their opinions
even when they are alone.

And when she wakes, this London minx
of seventeen, the whole city, the whole
Imperial rubbish heap of wastrels, scullions,
houris, fauns, and bedouin, will look to this
pillow where a life so young, secret, and clean
opens its eyes that it puts Mortality in doubt
– for possibly forty seconds.

The Flâneur and the Apocalypse

For his inebriated tread, the whole of Europe
With its great streets full of air and shade,
Its students and cocottes,
And traffic, roughly caked with blood,

Is not enough. The whole of Europe put to sleep
By music, coal-fires, snow, and café life,
And suffocated by hot fogs and poppies,
And rocked by lovers, like a chest of breath,

Is not, for the flâneur, drug strong enough.
A Europe…motionless with dust and night,
As if a squid her bag had emptied,
As if a doormat had been shaken over it,

Is not mysterious enough for his infatuated tread!
The Furies are modern, they don't drive you they entice
With cafés, lovers, dusty streets…with the Apocalypse
'Not this one – but the *next*,' they hiss.

Fear's Blindworm

Fear is the blindworm in the brain,
In souls that keep house with a dagger
And love the cabbage-shade,
Hell's brainworm gnaws the harder.

When God unpurses all the grudges
Of the Universe on lives propped up on crutches
Like a pier – seas rock to music
For years, before they break it into matches,

And all the roughly-handled blue lumber
Of the storm licks lightning and barks blood
At lives on their rough crutches made of timber,
And the soul is larder to Hell's worm of mud,

Then in the cabbage-cold underground of brains
Afraid of life, Eternity already has begun
When the worm turns Creation into dust
And the World crawls away from under them.

But pinched in the thighs of low duties,
Subject to forces that make Asia drag her anchor,
Souls that are *great* are in their element
Despite the feasting canker.

The Solitary's Bedroom

Now for the night, liquid or bristling!
When owls make the ink squeak at my window
And my bedroom that can bone my body of its will,
Drinks out my brains on pillows.
Like a bather caught and skinned by rollers
I shall toss for an eternity in surf,
When the air-eating spirit in my nostrils
Is maddened by its heavy coat of earth!

Now for your rest, eyes where my passions lay
Waterlogged in flashing muscles all day
Well below the waterline and plotted in their acids,
Salt mortice sets your lids.
Baked on Hell's rubbish heap I go on smouldering
With my spirit at its bread of breath
Incapable of beating out the flames! And hatches
Are raised cautiously by all the senses...

O once you have taken this draught of black air
You would be glad of infinity to get your bearings!

Rainfield and Argument

Pass on – to the next child, tranquil rainfield,
For this is the anthem
Of oblivion's white oxygen and bird warbling
In the abandoned rainfield
They sing who are disinherited.

And should the privileged fierce child deny
That all his rainfield hours
Belong to the Lord of oxygen and watershowers
And birds in deep rain resident,
Flutes of the clear firmament,

Then let him be dumbfounded by it *as a lie*;
Rainfields up to the knees
And hours that are ample and shimmering as seas
Are breath-taking and worthy
To be the work of Majesty.

And let him drown-bathe in the water firmament
That on webs rings a carillon
And birds that dress the breeze with wings, and own
They argue for the Lord of time
And white and icy oxygen.

Gutter Lord

I knew the poet's rag-soft eyelid was the gutter's fee
       For the way down to life. I had
       My lodgings in that quarter of the city
       Like a cat's ear full of cankered passages
Where November wraps the loiterer as spiders do their joints.

I was apprenticed to the moth bred from my clothes –
       Gold sail, folded up! for with
       Her tread, as Prince of footpads I could take
   My own grave unawares; or when my head was baked
With Jewish magic – stalk the Archangel, Thy *insect*, He

Whose nest is thatched to ride the juice and fire of storms!
       I was no merchant who for passport
       Strokes a pearl. Only those who trade
       Their rag-lid of bright lashes may business
In the Supernatural with the gutter for address.

My gutter – how you gleamed! Like dungeon floors which
       Cobras have lubricated
       Your time was kept in slimy yawns while you
       Prized up the warm roof of the poor man's shoe
And lacquered it with mire, that the grave might find

A way in to its meat – meanwhile the fool re-adored
       His face green as a toad
       Seen in a rippling crack of rain.
       The grave: whose grunt lifts the latch, whose
Leavings found at night upon my flank were as black bread

And smoked like Satan's droppings. O Heaven was greedy
    At my nostril dark as a violet
    To draw out her own breath from my brute
    Freeze it with winter while I slept, and
With it bolt me to the ground in linen and diamond!

Poet and Iceberg

No powerful and gloomy city,
Which has rid itself of vermin,
Will admit to keeping
One of these disreputable pets
With amorous limbs of milk
Fond of nocturnal strolls
And the immortal dirt of London
Under the clear panes of its nails.

Except the rogue is hunted off the street
And hissed, cities lie undefended
And weak from centuries of boredom
At the mercy of the pest
Who lives by thieving like all vermin
And will take a heart out of its chest
By force, and handle it
So gently that it's broken.

For brooding and embittered cities
Only slowly form their prejudice
Into an iceberg that is large enough
For ignorance to steer
From the bottom of a soul
By its rudder made of glass
Until the diamond smells blood and gores
The poet in the ribs in self-defence.

Oath

I swear that I would not go back
To pole the glass fishpools where the rough breath lies
That built the Earth – there, under the heavy trees
With their bark that's full of grocer's spice,

Not for an hour – although my heart
Moves, thirstily, to drink the thought – would I
Go back to run my boat
On the brown rain that made it slippery,

I would not for a youth
Return to ignorance, and be the wildfowl
Thrown about by the dark water seasons
With an ink-storm of dark moods against my soul,

And no firm ground inside my breast,
Only the breath of God that stirs
Scent-kitchens of refreshing trees,
And the shabby green cartilage of play upon my knees.

With no hard earth inside my breast
To hold a Universe made out of breath,
Slippery as fish with their wet mortar made of mirrors
I laid a grip of glass upon my youth.

And not for the waterpools would I go back
To a Universe unreal as breath – although I use
The great muscle of my heart
To thirst like a drunkard for the scent-storm of the trees.

Ace of Hooligans

Society on the globe. At first in here:
The sweet sour larder with its shelf of muslin bonnets
Fragile as kites, the Ace of Hooligans
Broke in his mouth to mutiny, a drink
Delicious as rain. While under his lashes of corn
The dream in fluent opal swam against his eyes
Its waters sumptuously baited as the sea
With chiffon nettles. O his gosling panes!
His zoo of sighs hot as a madman's breath,
Among blue smarting herbs and blue bee fur of rotten bread.

Outside: there was the ditch, the ideal boredom
In the brilliant thousands of a dose of thunderdrops;
The grass, smashed by the sky, which stews and tugs itself
On the muscular caramels of fast mud.
He, kneeling, with the moonlit sight of thieves,
Begged the ounce hog of the hedges she would seed
A touchy litter of her vermin commoners
That, gentle, he find syrup in his torn black mouth
Before the radiant traffic of space
Cut to pieces the palm of his hand.

Meadow giants, with hooks screwed to their bodies built of grass,
Their muzzles giving verbals of hot milk
Their ankles in the suck floor to a mucus climate,
These! When he raved for the globe's gilt side,
Sun forests' brute of fur, its blond swag head
Gorged at the warm beef of an earth hole, the red young stowed

Not twenty inches from the stupid boil of its nose.
The blue Male of the Equator, nude trunk
In war lacquers, throat groomed for hysteria.
While for divinity: the bronze Him roots out the white It.

Still a cipher, with a name sewn to his clothes,
Sexless as trout or chestnut eaten when the flesh is green,
He crossed the salt stare of the chart, its groping margins;
Land, clothed in steam, whose sea lisps to its pod of monsters;
Those plains where heaven thrums the blades grilled light as foil,
And tows the stallion, flash neck and nude-lipped head,
On burnt white hair. Whole skies shantung and music
In the tree drunk with his weather! the foreigner,
His merchandise rahat lacoum in fragrant drums
To trade the Irish who speak water on the syllable.

Beasts lit their eyes; the planet took in moth and dog.
Across the rubbishy beloved continent
Was drawn the circus with its tinsel hutch of midgets;
Fluorescent tournaments of ladylike brown animals,
He smelt man's acid in their tame wool coats.
Hair as bright as butter scorched his boyhood chin,
A vein painted and roped against his thigh,
And his mouth felt her tongue. Returning home
His dazzled body hunted Africa
The red yes at the top of six flights of stairs.

The blind rubbers of the mouth of love!
The awakening with citron stare!
Morning: in a sty of tinted women.
She, on a quilt, bit roses; mammal pink.

He, a witch scab on his dream, left for infinity
While his soul peered out of his navel, hideous.
Streets: uttering bull smoke. Under a wall
Slum vegetable, its meat leg feeding.
His arrogance, these nerves which focus ecstasy –
Accelerations of the bankrupt mud.

The light; sashes and lustres. The crammed and rustling ball.
A dog rinsing its jaws in the sweet juice of a lake.
O thigh purring against raiment! O treacherous
No man's land.

Rome

It's the café and the boredom, in the semi-dark
People have a certain rank elegance
And the dirt-encrusted street with its great jar of water
Keeps my blood too fresh and truculent for work.

All these Roman fops going by, the shuffling,
The dripping waterjar and the dark café
...built for stealing people...
And the walls are full of musk, it's baked into them.

The temptation to live! Even a bad conversation...
In a street that's built for boredom
And odorous with water. When there's less time
(My life, my work, my hopes!) every step leads to an assignation.

It's the élan of café life on a hot night,
The street that's full of modern love-talk, like a room,
It's the jade-breath of the waterjar...that is mortality
For the blood that is too insolent for work.

Hypnos and Warm Winters

Europe is all steam and leaves and love-affairs!
Old streets – they're bathrooms of steam and water
Where Hypnos follows me all day in a silk dressing-gown,
Like two old bores we move through the great months of rain.

Suppose I'm coming from my love-affair...
While the steam-heated rain pours down,
And yawning takes the wax and starch out of my skin,

It's the last straw having to describe the night
Again in detail to my heart – as if it wasn't there,

When Hypnos, like a twentieth-century bachelor
Bored easily, is lying full length on my bed
– With the effrontery to add to his art the spice
Of fanning me to sleep – with sheets of my own verse.

Escape!

It is among the bins and dormitories of cities
Where the busker wins his bread
By turning music on a spit, and the heavens
Have the dirt of the great sty upon their sides,

That one goes to gormandise upon Escape!
Where alleys are so narrow that the Fates
Like meatporters can scarcely pass
With their awkward burden in its muslin bandages,

And carry off the rabble safely to their graves;
Where every shadow opens a bordel
At sunset, as decay moves
Into cloakrooms of blue velvet in red cheese;

These are the last of the great kitchens!
And your soul knows half the flavour
Lies underfoot in dirty flagstones,
When like a chef it makes a point of bringing in

To show before you dine – Escape,
Still active in a net,
Auroras, icy champagnes upon its wings!

Story of a Hotel Room

Thinking we were safe – insanity!
We went in to make love. All the same
Idiots to trust the little hotel bedroom.
Then in the gloom...
...And who does not know that pair of shutters
With the awkward hook on them
All screeching whispers? Very well then, in the gloom
We set about acquiring one another
Urgently! But on a temporary basis
Only as guests – just guests of one another's senses.

But idiots to feel so safe you hold back nothing
Because the bed of cold, electric linen
Happens to be illicit....
To make love as well as that is ruinous.
Londoner, Parisian, someone should have warned us
That without permanent intentions
You have absolutely no protection
– If the act is clean, authentic, sumptuous,
The concurring deep love of the heart
Follows the naked work, profoundly moved by it.

Bedouin of the London Evening

Ten years in your cafés and your bedrooms
Great city, filled with wind and dust!

Bedouin of the London evening,
On the way to a restaurant my youth was lost.

And like a medium who falls into a trance
So deep, she can be scratched to death
By her Familiar – at its leisure!
I have lain rotting in a dressing-gown
While being savaged (horribly) by wasted youth.

I have been young too long, and in a dressing-gown
My private modern life has gone to waste.

Boy in the Lane

in search of origin

This lane at zenith; when its hair is warm.
Here's the magician with his Pedigree of Snouts
Whose ransack shimmers after him.
And here's the lair in music trousseau where his lout's
Foot beat out a bright bed. The Atlas stuffs his shoes
With tussore. A dark animal
Pulls August out of the hedge, the linctus dropping as it chews,
Eyes him with the clear gog of Lucifer, the edible
Hot silk of the dream pasture in its mouth.

Geography lays eggs and pearls.

Thirst! And the ceiling advances with luminous hulls.
Panes of weather are left flashing in the path;
Quagmarks of angels in the mud,
The blue thrash of the Jesus fairy. And the youth
Detonates this spoor to drive the Magnifico in thud
And glare of blades against his ear;
The heavenly quops vamped by the tender oilskin of the drum!
His breast reports the code, as a snake dines off some rare
Tattoo its literate satin muscle cannot name.

Archbrute of quadrillion Kingbeats!

But the north flies a magnetic blue roan cloud
Whose touchwaters on the scented dirt of the sphere
Set – in jay's wing fathoms. And Mud
Looks up through this aquarium of rain, from her
Queasy seance under the grope of the great knotted lips
Of riverpike, whose tarnished flesh
Drinks the umber hangings of the bottom. This boy who clips
Himself a Dynasty of Wings – is hers! Hers to the ghost rash
On his lily-clapping vellum, that strokes her lie to death.

Fog Peacocks

We were the city's young, and our veins
If they ran pale from the bad food
Even so they carried the infernos of its moods,
For we were the children of the rotting peacock
Of a passer-by, seen in a mist of scorching bitumen.

Oh you bound homeward when the cloud
Of gold gas shone behind the house,
With a captured insect, once half Helium
Now only spurs and gauze,
And the green liquor pool in jars of glass...

We were not less whose city like an alcohol
Spoke hotly to the artery; and we already
Knew love's streets – where at the fall
Of thermal, phosphorescent dusk
There is a drop that goes down sheer to Hell.

Those evenings you were mutinous
Against the tyranny of kitchen tables where
The flat iron cools its mirror of blue ore
And grip of hot rag,
And the old blanket smokes like humus,

We were the young, derisive metropolitans
Soon to be mashed flat as a wet coalsack by skies
Of ochre, full of malice, coating the trees with emulsion,
And you would have to drag for our disgust in sewers,
And break the cobwebs reaching an illusion.

Poet as Gambler

Now like a gambler on an errand
Of my wasted youth, when gutter and heavens
Were my lottery, and my estate
A shirt of water-lotus that the night wind

Loved to rock as I went to do my gambling
Alone at dusk in the dark city
To out-bid Eternity – with nothing
But a blouse of lilies flooding my lapel

A wallet stuffed with fever for my stake,
All night until the early hours when stowaways
Will grope for the unknown and illustrate
Their clothes with lustrous bruises as they go aboard

And all the ropes and fabrics of a boat
Are heavy with cold nectars in the dawn,
Creation, glimmering and surly underfoot,
And Egypt drowsy on a cake of opium,

I went with nothing but the shirt upon my back
To cast lots with the Infinite,
And my bid was the blouse that rocks
On gamblers with a linen sail all night.

Apprentice

to the lane, the zephyr, and the east.

There is no scholarship to lane and zephyr
Like a boorish, pampered youth!
I have no documents to hawk – sinner and loafer
In the airy darkness – but on a London night
When boats lie up with jewelled nostrils, and under
Sheets of dust and satin, water is in slumber,

Inquire of my ability to be last off the streets
When I am molten, stupid, dangerous,
Under an alley's aspic wall with bullying confederates
In arms, love, lies, and law-breakings.
And for my knowledge of the dawn
Examine me upon the solitary power-drunk return

From the nocturnal city; walking when the world
Is marvellous, upon a country road
My boot – that's plump with mildew and uncorseted –
The first to tread the lane when it is dug out
Fresh and dripping from the ether, and the spade
Laid by – heavenly crust still luminous upon it!

Delinquent! with bedlam's pulses sobbing in my limbs
And tomorrow – all gold bruises
On the rise! Test me (while I am fresh from sins
And villainy) upon the conduct of the zephyr
At the hour he leaves the atmosphere to join the finches
In the path, and wash his fresh wings in the dust.

You, who would tame with toolbag or certificate
My shudder... as the east
Drinks diamonds, and the world's born blazing underfoot!
Surgeon and robber learn their touch in the great city,
But I am after heavenly spoil, and it is
As a gloveless trespasser that I desire supremacy.

Blouson Noir

And the revolutionary – half-drugged by the wet trees
In Paris in low spirits moves on
Through the scent-kilns full of gnats
He'll be ruined – his throat rots with happiness.

They're dirty like a lodging-house, the waterfronts,
But the dust is seductive to him
The jasmine atmosphere and hot drip of the thunder
That crushes Paris bone by bone.

Zut! He can hear modern life going on!
Who lives off the sight of a Paris street!
Down here, it's dark as a medicine,
It's April – everything anointed and caked.

And his malaise is fabulous....
The dirt beds of the trees and the hot dust!
It's lethal to patrol here, brainsick and odious,
On the alluring quays he's rotten with happiness.

Bedouin of the London Morning

We come into the café at dawn,
There are waterfogs, and civilisation is white
...if you knew the exotic disgust that grips me

After another bestial night
As we come in, broken; dark with inks and dusts and gases
Like those whose private apartment is the street.

After an all-night conversation
When the street-wind hangs on snarling to your coat,
If you knew my (half erotic) convulsion of loathing

For the night. (I'm like a sleeper
When his mouth is stopped up
By some terrible mud-crust the dream has crammed there

And the soul goes pressing up against
Trying to scream with hydrophobia – and can only murmur.
Some love-thought turns his mouth to blood with longing

Only a moment later.) In the workman's café
If you knew the almost voluptuous sense of frustration
When you're broken... And the morning's alcoholic as a lily.

April and the Ideas-Merchant

I was plying my trade in the street,
It was a rainy agate twilight
And my eyes were half lid...but my town-bred soul
Was tempted and within an inch of giving in.

I was at work upon a suburb of my brain,
An ultra-treacherous idea was in its private room there
And I was closing in – with the ink streaming off my brow!
But my soul attentive to the agate oxygen.

Crates of glass and water had been dumped down by the weather,
Overhead a last skylight opened in the Koh-i-noor
– A whole civilisation was loose, bully and vixen
Moving along, roasting hot, ready for anything!

And – odium – I was in the chien-loup
Of the Latin Quarter of my brain
Where certain dark yellow hours go by
...that lead off surreptitiously into eternity.

Academic! Hack! Vulgarian!
You mistook the nature of your calling. Poets are only at work,
With an agate daylight going through the street,
When they live, dream, *bleed* – within an inch of giving in to art.

On the advantage of being ill-treated by the World

I have a quarrel with the world
At music in my breast
To walk the shabby thrilling twilight of the street
And to be stewed in fogs that stick
To me, as a tramp's nest
All lice and dews, sticks to his clothes...

Rouses my soul to beat the velvet sinews
Of her thickets! To bear
Old toothmarks bitten deep into my side
Where January can always fit his blade
And halve me with the saw
Again, like sorcerers, while *living*...

Goads my invisible to cuff her instrument
My breast! To stoop and grow
Hard callouses where the black weather
Rests its knuckles on me like a sulky Pasha
Upon the brow
Of his pet slave, grating magnificent rings...

Makes my tenant thunder my complaint
Upon her velvet ropes!
And yet... as powerful but indolent composers
Will only work when bailiffs pound their doors,
Where my musician lodges
I need Adversity to break its claws!

Iliad of Broken Sentences

(1967)

Since the publication of *Notes on Cafés and Bedrooms* Rosemary Tonks has moved steadily forward in her search for a diction which allows the material objects, the sensibility, and the humour of today to be incorporated naturally inside the framework of a visionary modern lyric. Her poetry has a dramatic but spontaneous texture, enabling it to carry vast and timeless themes lightly within it; and by qualifying and nourishing these themes with contemporary experience she gains for them new emotional, visual, and moral dimensions. The deserts of the Middle-East are again equated with city life; and this is a handbook to its sofas, hotel corridors, cinemas, underworlds, cardboard suitcases, self-willed buses, banknotes, soapy bathrooms, pork-filled newspapers – and to its anguish, its enraged excitement, its great lonely joys.

Jacket note, *Iliad of Broken Sentences* (The Bodley Head, 1967)

The Sofas, Fogs, and Cinemas

I have lived it, and lived it,
My nervous, luxury civilisation,
My sugar-loving nerves have battered me to pieces.

...Their idea of literature is hopeless.
Make them drink their own poetry!
Let them eat their gross novel, full of mud.

It's quiet; just the fresh, chilly weather...and he
Gets up from his dead bedroom, and comes in here
And digs himself into the sofa.
He stays there up to two hours in the hole – and talks
– Straight into the large subjects, he faces up to *everything*
It's......damnably depressing.
(That great lavatory coat...the cigarillo burning
In the little dish... And when he calls out: 'Ha!'
Madness! – you no longer possess your own furniture.)

On my bad days (and I'm being broken
At this very moment) I speak of my ambitions...and he
Becomes intensely gloomy, with the look of something jugged,
Morose, sour, mouldering away, with lockjaw....

I grow coarser; and more modern (*I*, who am driven mad
By my ideas; who go nowhere;
Who dare not leave my frontdoor, lest an idea...)
All right. I admit everything, everything!

Oh yes, the opera (Ah, but the cinema)
He particularly enjoys it, enjoys it *horribly*, when someone's ill
At the last minute; and they specially fly in
A new, gigantic, Dutch soprano. He wants to help her
With her arias.   Old goat! Blasphemer!
He wants to help her with her arias!

No, I...go to the cinema,
I particularly like it when the fog is thick, the street
Is like a hole in an old coat, and the light is brown as laudanum.
...the fogs! the fogs! The cinemas
Where the criminal shadow-literature flickers over our faces,
The screen is spread out like a thundercloud – that bangs
And splashes you with acid...or lies derelict, with lighted
              waters in it,
And in the silence, drips and crackles – taciturn, luxurious.
... The drugged and battered Philistines
Are all around you in the auditorium...

And he...is somewhere else, in his dead bedroom clothes,
He wants to make me think his thoughts
And they will be *enormous*, dull – (just the sort
To keep away from).
...when I see that cigarillo, when I see it...smoking
And he wants to face the international situation...
Lunatic rages! Blackness! Suffocation!

– All this sitting about in cafés to calm down
Simply wears me out. And their idea of literature!
The idiotic cut of the stanzas; the novels, full up, gross.

I have lived it, and I know too much.
My café-nerves are breaking me
With black, exhausting information.

The Sash Window

Outside that house, I stood like a dog;
The window was mysterious, with its big, dull pane
Where the mud pastes are thrown by dark, alkaline skies
That glide slowly along, keeping close to the ground.

– But for the raging disgust which shook me
So that my throat was scratched by her acid
(Whose taste is the true Latin of culture) –
I could have lived the life of these roads.

That piece of filthy laurel moves up and down,
And then the dead rose-leaves with their spat-on look
Where the sour carbon lies...under
The sash of the window comes the smell of stewing innards,

With the freshly washed lavatory – I know where
The old linoleum has its platinum wet patches
And the disinfectant dries off in whiffs.
Hellish, abominable house where I have been young!

With your insane furnishings – above all
The backs of dressing-tables where the dredged wood
Faces the street, raw. And the window
With its servant-maid's mystery, which contains *nothing*,

Where I bowed over the ruled-up music books
With their vitreous pencilling, and the piano keys
That touched water. How forlornly my strong, destructive head
Eats again the reek of the sash window.

Epoch of the Hotel Corridor

I understand you, frightful epoch,
With your jampots, brothels, paranoias,
And your genius for fear, you can't stop shuddering.
Discothèques, I drown among your husky, broken sentences.

I know that to get through to you, my epoch,
I must take a diamond and scratch
On your junkie's green glass skin, my message
And my joy – sober, piercing, twilit.

In the hotel where you live, my Kurdish epoch,
Your opera of typewriters and taperecorders
Boils the hotel with a sumptuous oompah!
...(...as my heavy-drinking diamond writes)

Boils it! And loosens the bread-grey crusts
Of stucco from the 19th Century...with an opera
Of broken, twilit poetry
Built from your dust-drowned underworld of sighs.

Epoch, we are lonely. For we follow hotel berbers
Of the past, those who drift in corridors, whose tents
And whose derisive manuscripts are dipped in marble
By your backward glance.

Badly-chosen Lover

Criminal, you took a great piece of my life,
And you took it under false pretences,
That piece of time
– In the clear muscles of my brain
I have the lens and jug of it!
Books, thoughts, meals, days, and houses,
Half Europe, spent like a coarse banknote,
You took it – leaving mud and cabbage stumps.

And, Criminal, I damn you for it (very softly).
My spirit broke her fast on you. And, Turk,
You fed her with the breath of your neck
– In my brain's clear retina
I have the stolen love-behaviour.
Your heart, greedy and tepid, brothel-meat,
Gulped it, like a flunkey with erotica.
And very softly, Criminal, I *damn* you for it.

The Little Cardboard Suitcase

Events pushed me into this corner;
I live in a fixed routine,
With my cardboard attaché case full of rotting books.
...If only I could trust my blood! Those damn foreign women
Have a lot to answer for, marrying into the family –

– The mistakes, the wrong people, the half-baked ideas,
And their beastly comments on everything. Foul.
But irresistibly amusing, that is the whole trouble.

With my cardboard suitcase full of occidental literature
I reached this corner, to educate myself
Against the sort of future they flung into my blood –
The events, the people, the ideas – the *ideas*!
And I alone know how disreputable and foreign.

But as a thinker, as a professional water-cabbage,
From my desk, of course, I shall dissolve events
As if they were of no importance ... none whatever.

...And those women are to blame!
I was already half-way into my disreputable future,
When I found that they had thrown into my blood
With the mistakes, the people, the ideas (ideas indeed!)
This little cardboard suitcase ... damned
Beloved women ... and these books, opium, beef, God.

At my desk (lit by its intellectual cabbage-light)
I found them – and they are irresistibly amusing –
These thoughts that have been thrown into my blood.

Hydromaniac

I was leaning across your chest;
Like a marble-smith, I made pencilmarks over
Its vanilla skin, its young man's skin,
Refreshing as the pleasure page in a daily newspaper.
I sniffed you to quench my thirst,
As one sniffs in the sky huge, damp sheets of lightning
That bring down the chablis, hocks, moselles,
And tear cold, watery holes.
Those soaking wet chords from Brahms (...their overflow,
On which you could float a canoe)
Are not more refreshing! Nor is the fragrant gin-fizz
From the glass joint of a rod of grass.

My life cries out for water!
Haughty sheets of newsprint, lightning, music, skin!
Haughty bathrooms where the lukewarm swimmer
In his water-colour coat of soap is king.

Students in Bertorelli's

Winter! We pour our politics into the brown walls,
These little eating-houses run with grease like a meat chop.
Each man stuffs himself with ideas, he eats his pork newspaper.
With two or three cabbage banknotes you can listen to the fog-horn,
The striking of the great clocks (how terrible), the alarm-bells,
      without fear.

We are ready to slide away into the nearest gutter,
Like old Paris hotels the fogs won't leave in peace,
In the souks where the young pair off, dog-tired and dirty,
On a February evening...
Nothing holds us upright but some cold green diction, banknotes,
      a penis.
And they talk of Literature!

But after all, give me again that new green diction.
Oh yes, it's atrocious. Certainly it's literature.

The Desert Wind Élite

I am outside life, and pour the sand
For my own desert, *recklessly*.
But if some flame splashes over from my arab hours
Into your dismal, shadow-bathing century...

...And burns you, gutter-polished citizen,
With my story – the drifting novocain of my horizon,
My oases, and my mirages, they're built of tears
And sheets and sheets of grey glass like an onion,

My story written in the sand! Laziness, despair,
Worldly pressures, travelling, & dirty clothes, the need for sleep,
Contempt for time – and more despair. Oh yes; I'm a writer
Daring enough to make the sand my paper,

It's done by *living*, ignoramuses. Isn't there always
The unreliability, the cool mouth-bite of a beloved body?
That's the desert – where I hurry!...slowly, very slowly,
Sometimes...almost stock-still in a sand-drift...hurrying.

While dusty mobs pass, driven by the moon.
...If it blasts you, modernists fobbed off
With dingy souls, inside a century that growls
For its carafe of shady air, oblivion, and psychiatric mash,

Start Drinking! I shall seduce you. From my desk,
The Soho of my drifting, yellowed sentences
Calls out your name... Choked-up joy splashes over
From this poem and you're crammed, stuffed to the brim, at dusk,

With hell's casual and jam-green happiness!!
Ah, pour yourself a desert, man-in-the-shadow-skin.
This last minute enamel re-satanises Europe,
And you will become my arab and my citizen.

*   *   *

I was walking in this shadow-bathing century
Pouring sand for my own desert
From my desolate high spirits...
......but *recklessly*, my arab and my citizen.

An Old-fashioned Traveller on the Trade Routes

I was sitting upstairs in a bus, cursing the waste of time, and pouring my life away on one of those insane journeys across London – while gradually the wavering motion of this precarious glass salon, that flung us about softly like trusses of wheat or Judo Lords, began its medicinal work inside the magnetic landscape of London.

The bus, with its transparent decks of people, trembled. And was as uniquely ceremonious in propelling itself as an eminent Jellyfish with an iron will, by expulsions, valves, hisses, steams, and emotional respirations. A militant, elementary, caparisoned Jellyfish, of the feminine sex, systematically eating and drinking the sea.

I began to feel as battered as though I had been making love all night! My limbs distilled the same interesting wide-awake weariness.

We went forward at a swimmer's pace, gazing through the walls that rocked the weather about like a cloudy drink from a chemist's shop – with the depth and sting of the Baltic. The air-shocks, the sulphur dioxides, the gelatin ignitions! We were all of us parcelled up in mud-coloured clothes, dreaming, while the rich perishable ensemble – as stuffy and exclusive as a bag of fish and chips, or as an Eskimo's bed in a glass drift – cautiously advanced as though on an exercise from a naval college.

The jogging was so consistently idiotic, it induced a feeling of complete security. I gave up my complicated life on the spot; and lay screwed up like an old handkerchief screwed up in a pocket, suspended in time, ready to go to the ends of the earth. O trans-Siberian railways! Balloons! Astronauts!

The Ice-cream Boom Towns

Hurry: we must go south to escape
The bubonic yellow-drink of our old manuscripts,
You, with your career, toad-winner, I with my intolerance.
The English seacoast is more oafish than a ham.

We can parade together softly, aloof
Like envoys in coloured clothes – on the promenades,
The stone sleeping-tables where the bourgeois bog down,
And the brilliant sea swims vigorously in and out.

There will be hot-house winds to blunt themselves
Against the wooden bathing-huts, and fall down senseless;
Lilos that swivel in the shallow, iced waves, half-submerged;
Skiffs – trying to bite into a sea that's watertight!

One whiff of it – careerist – and we fall down senseless,
Bivouacked! Your respirating, steep, electric head,
Filled by its nervous breakdown, will slumber narcotised
By the clear gas that trembles in the sandpit.

Under the pier will be an overdose of shadows – the Atlantic
Irrigates the girders with enormous, disembodied cantos,
Unless you're quick – they pull the clothes off your soul
To make it moan some watery, half-rotten stanzas.

Night! The plasterboard hotels that rattle shanty bedrooms
On the front, are waiting! Without gods, books, sex or family,
We'll sink to a vast depth, and lie there, musing, interlocked
Like deportees who undulate to phosphorescent booming.

Addiction to an Old Mattress

No, this is not my life, thank God...
...worn out like this, and crippled by brain-fag;
Obsessed first by one person, and then
(Almost at once) most horribly besotted by another;
These Februaries, full of draughts and cracks,
They belong to the people in the streets, the others
Out there – haberdashers, writers of menus.

Salt breezes! Bolsters from Istanbul!
Barometers, full of contempt, controlling moody isobars.
Sumptuous tittle-tattle from a summer crowd
That's fed on lemonades and matinées. And seas
That float themselves about from place to place, and then
Spend *hours* – just moving some clear sleets across glass stones.
Yalta: deck-chairs in Asia's gold cake; thrones.

Meanwhile... I live on...powerful, disobedient,
Inside their draughty haberdasher's climate,
With these people...who are going to obsess me,
Potatoes, dentists, people I hardly know, it's unforgivable
For this is not my life
But theirs, that I am living.
And I wolf, bolt, gulp it down, day after day.

Song of the October Wind

A mighty air-sea, fierce and very clean,
Was gliding in across the city.
Oxygenating gusts swept down and
Chloroformed us, in a light too bright to see by.

On pavements – china and milk pages
In a good book, freshly iced by the printing press –
October flash-floated. And you and I were moving
With alert, sane, and possessive steps. At home,

My sofa wrote her creaking, narcoleptic's Iliad.
My bathroom drank the Styx (bathwater
Of the Underworld). My telephone took all its voices
And gave them to the Furies, to practise with.

While slowly – to gigantic, muddy blows of music
From a pestle and mortar – roof, floor, walls, doors,
My London, stuffed with whisky-dark hotels,
Began to pant like a great ode!

And threw, carelessly, into our veins
Information – all the things we needed to know,
For which there are no words, *not even thoughts*.
And this was an ode shaken from a box of rats.

The first sky from October's aviary
Of bone-dry, thudding skies, joyful, free, and young,
With its wings lifted our souls, heavy as cities,
Effortlessly. We were trustworthy again.

Ritz, Savoy, Claridge's, hotels full of peacock words,
Were beaten white by Boreas; and as
Electric frosts scratched the windows
Fitting in their awkward childish pane of glowing stone,

We – copied the foaming *with our souls*!
The same ode tore the streets inside us. And lit
Catwalks, sofas, taxis in that city with a light
So bright, even the blind could see by it.

Done for!

Take care whom you mix with in life, irresponsible one,
For if you mix with the wrong people
– And you yourself may be one of the wrong people –
If you make love to the wrong person,

In some old building with its fabric of dirt,
As clouds of witchcraft, nitro-glycerine, and cake,
Brush by (one autumn night) still green
From our green sunsets...and then let hundreds pass, unlit,

They will do you ferocious, indelible harm!
Far beyond anything you can imagine, jazzy sneering one,
And afterwards you'll live in no man's land,
You'll lose your identity, and never get yourself back, diablotin,

It may have happened already, and as you read this...
Ah, it *has* happened already. I remember, in an old building;
Clouds which had cut themselves on a sharp winter sunset
(With its smoking stove of frosts to keep it cold) went by,
          bleeding.

Orpheus in Soho

His search is desperate!
And the little night-shops of the Underworld
With their kiosks...they know it,
The little bars as full of dust as a stale cake,
None of these places would exist without Orpheus
And how well they know it.

...when the word goes ahead to the next city,
An underworld is hastily constructed,
With bitch-clubs, with cellars and passages,
So that he can go on searching, desperately!

As the brim of the world is lit,
And breath pours softly over the Earth,
And as Heaven moves ahead to the next city
With deep airs, and with lights and rains,

He plunges into Hades, for his search is desperate!
And there is so little risk...down there,
That is the benefit of searching frenziedly
Among the dust-shops and blind-alleys
...there is so little risk of finding her
In Europe's old blue Kasbah, and he knows it.

Dressing-gown Olympian

I *insist* on vegetating here
In motheaten grandeur. Haven't I plotted
Like a madman to get here? Well then.

These free days, these side-streets,
Mouldy or shiny, with their octoroon light;
Also, I have grudges, enemies, a religion,
Politics, a new morality – everything!

Kept awake by alcohol and coffee,
Inside her oriental dressing-gown of dust
My soul is always thinking things over, thoroughly.
No wonder my life has grandeur, depth, and crust.

Ah, to desire a certain way of life,
And then to gain it!
What a mockery, what absolute misery,
Dressing-gown hours the tint of alcohol or coffee.

Am I an imbecile of the first water after all?
Yes, I think I can claim – now that all this grandeur,
Depth, and crust is stacked around me – that I am.

Farewell to Kurdistan

As my new life begins, I start smiling at the people around me,
You would think I'd just been given a substantial meal,
I see all their good points.
The railway sheds are full of greenish-yellow electricity,
It's the great midday hour in London...that suddenly goes brown.
...My stupefying efforts to make money
And to have a life!
Well, I'm leaving; nothing can hold me.

The platforms are dense to the foot,
Rich, strong-willed travellers pace about in the dark daylight,
And how they stink of green fatty soaps, the rich.
More dirty weather...you can hardly see the newspaper stand
With its abominable, ludicrous papers...which are so touching
I ought to laugh and cry, instead of gritting my teeth.

Let me inhale the filthy air for the last time,
Good heavens, how vile it is.... I could take you step by step
Back among the twilight buildings, into my old life...

The trains come in, boiling, caked!
The station half tames them, there's the sound of blows; the
    uproar!
And I – I behave as though I've been starved of noise,
My intestine eats up this big music
And my new bourgeois soul promptly bursts into flames, in
    mid-air.

No use pouring me a few last minutes of the old life
From your tank of shadow, filled with lost and rotten people,
I admit: the same flow of gutter-sugar to the brain...
I admit it, London.

No one to see me off – Ah!
I would like to be seen off; it must be the same agonising woman
Who does not want to understand me, and who exposes me
          in public,
So that I can turn away, choked with cold bile,
And feel myself loved absolutely; the bitch.

These carriages, that have the heavy brown and black bread
Up their sides! But look out for the moment of cowardice,
It's Charon's rowing-boat that lurches and fouls my hand
As I climb on – exile, Limboist.

...The way these people get on with their lives; I bow down
With my few deeds and my lotus-scars.
Last minutes...last greenish-yellow minutes
Of the lost and rotten hours...faro, and old winters dimmed,
On which the dark – Yes, the black sugar-crust is forming,
          London.

I'm leaving! Nothing can hold me!
The trains, watered and greased, scream to be off.
Hullo – I'm already sticking out my elbows for a piece of
          territory,
I occupy my place as though I can't get enough of it
– And with what casual, haughty, and specific gestures, incidentally.

Tradesmen, Pigs, regenerative trains – I shall be saved!
I shall go to the centre of Europe; gliding,
As children skate on the diamond lid of the lake
Never touching ground – Xenophile, on the blue-plated meadows.

Oh I shall live off myself, rainclothes, documents,
The great train simmers.... Life is large, large!
...I shall live off your loaf of shadows, London;
I admit it, at the last.

Black Kief and the Intellectual

I shall fill up that pit inside me
With my gloomiest thoughts; and then
Spread myself, prostrate, inert, on top of them.
Ah, miserable at last! Felicity.
Those who drink the sea with its fishy breath
Cannot know with what dread I gorge to death
On ideologies – bitter dogma, dialectic, creed;
H.P. sauce, ketchup, mayonnaise, chutney,
Filthy kitchen work that swindles, that says 'feed',
Dried-up certitude, monkish inhibition, duty,
That helps us to fall downhill, mad as swine.
There, alone, I see my obligation. But let me begin
By describing my tiredness…a word on my depression.

The Drinkers of Coffee

We talk openly, and exchange souls.
Power-shocks of understanding knock us off our feet!
The same double life among the bores and vegetables,
By lamplight in the coffee-houses you have sat it out
Half toad, half Sultan, of the rubbish-heap,
You know the deadly dull excitement; the champagne sleet
Of living; you know all the kitchen details of my ego's thinking,
When, with our imaginations shuddering,
We move arrogantly into one another's power,
And the last barriers go down between us....

More at home in a jazz pit than with you,
Hotter on the Baltic, when it fries in ice,
Better understood by cattle, grocers, blocks of wood,
My refrigerated body feels the coffin's touch in every word
You utter, and backs away for ever from your bed.
You know me far too well, O dustbin of the soul;
My sex, her nerve completely broken by it, has constructed
Barriers, thick walls, never to be battered down.
On the other side (with a last mouthful of the double-dutch to spit!)
She looks away; and in a wholly opposite direction.

To a Certain Young Man
(or The Carrier-bag Eros)

I can hear the Eros of grey rain, Veganin, and telephones
Inside your voice.
His wings, once cut out of Greek frost,
Are now the tint of an old, polished street.

Softly croaking out clichés, in the narrow passage
With its gas-pipes and fuse-boxes, he makes us
Zoophytes – sponging up gravy, nightmares, dullness!
We fill our veins with soapy water, anxious

To be good enough...for this latrine whore, Eros.
Always, Arabia Desetta; the solitary table
In the restaurant is where we end up,
At the mercy of a salt and pepper pot.

Hosanna! I accept, without quibbling, fly-scrawl,
The carrier-bag of cheap sentences,
On these terms, unless...there is a way to lower them.
I accept. For *my* Eros is atrocious....

If water-clear moonlight and streets
Sharper than greengages are your drink,
Drunkard, you can be cured. One wound from Eros
And your breast can only drink arrows

With its illiterate and fragrant mud,
(Teetotaller, dead drunk on your own blood.)
It's ludicrous! It's hopeless.
Shut up your underworlds! Close your hearts!

The century is over. Doors are slamming
In the tragic, casual era. The Eros of dead café tunes
Is in your voice....
He salts and peppers me another pair of arms.

A Few Sentences Away

What a night! My past is very close.
Dark rag-and-satin April in the city
Moves its water-lily breezes, one by one. My fading letters!
My café-au-lait sentences that groaned for love and money.

There are nights when...
Lying an inch or two above the ground inside my head,
Heavy, but rippling with levitations, philosophy's
Bokhara carpet flies my past in and out of Time.

My past, no older than an April night!
A few streets away – boulevard scab of a hotel
She lived in; her armchair voyages inside a bottle;
Her pride, its great sciatic nerve ready at a word to –

......England is darker than a thrush, tonight,
Brown, trustworthy hours lie ahead. Suddenly
My past hurls her dream towards me!
I steady myself:...but how tender, carnal, blasé it is.

Let me *hide*, well away from a past that dreams
Like that. Away from streets that taste of blood & sugar
When the glowing month smashes itself against the hedges
In the dark. I need ink poured by an abbey;

For...April, old greengrocer, I throw ahead of me a universe
Above your dripping clouds in flames, below
The deep, opulent engorgement of your soul in rut; & so lasting
Time snatches its hours there, like a poppy, when it can.

Selected Prose

Note on *Notes on Cafés and Bedrooms*

My foremost preoccupation at the moment is the search for an idiom which is individual, contemporary and musical. And one that has sufficient authority to bear the full weight of whatever passion I would wish to lay upon it.

Every poet who has been confined – at the mercy of form when he has come of age emotionally – and has found half the things he wants to say well out of his poem's range, knows the immensity of the task. And I am not speaking here of metrical skills, but of absolute freshness and authenticity in handling diction.

What I write about must develop from my life and times. I am especially conscious of the great natural forces which bring modern life up to date. My concern here is with exact emotional proportions – proportions as they are now current for me. Ideally, whatever is heightened should be justified both by art and by life; while the poet remains vulnerable to those moments when a poem suddenly makes its own terms – and with an overwhelming force that is self-justifying. For this reason certain poetic ideas have little validity when lifted out of context. I am consequently uneasy when discussing the logic of a poem with those whose intellectual equipment is purely mathematical. If you say that the English have a love of order which is puritanical, and the French a love of order which is imaginative, that does not make one more orderly than the other. The progress of feeling in a poem may be no less logical than the development of argument.

Telling the truth about feeling requires prodigious integrity. Most people can describe a chest of drawers, but a state of mind is more resistant. A hackneyed metaphor is the first sign of a compromise with intention; your reader damns you instantly, and though he may read on with his senses, you have lost his heart. Some poets do manage to converge on their inner life by generating emotion from an inspired visual imagery; in this instance the images exist in their own right, but may be thought to be in a weaker position as the raw material of the emotion in preference to a larger existence as illustration of it.

Poetry Book Society Bulletin (Spring 1963)

Interview with Peter Orr

TONKS: I think it diabolical, this getting of a poet out of his or her back room and the making of them into public figures who have to give opinions every twenty seconds. I know this is what the French do, but I don't approve of it.

ORR: You don't think it helps, do you, for a poet to talk direct to his public, otherwise than through his poetry?

TONKS: Well, I avoid this on every possible occasion, first of all because it means a loss of something like two weeks' work, during which time I worry about it, and then I get over it. When one is writing one is an introvert, and when one goes on to a stage one must make oneself into an extrovert.

ORR: Unless, I suppose, one is a Dylan Thomas kind of person who enjoys that sort of thing enormously?

TONKS: Yes, but it killed him eventually, the enormous strain of each performance, for a man who was both, of course, but who found it progressively more strenuous and who wrote less and less poetry, so that every time he went on the stage he knew that he was giving up another poem, practically, which he could have written. You either read and you give talks and you become a public person, or else you write consistently and every day and think on a certain level. You can't go back to that deep level of thinking if you are too much a social person.

ORR: Does this deep level of thinking preclude the idea of an audience?

TONKS: I could communicate if only the English weren't quite so English, but you know they don't finish their sentences; and anyway they are not passionately concerned with their subject, and so the conversation tends to turn into a series of already-hammered-out academic platitudes, which means to say you are not going to break fresh ground, you are only going to exchange academies.

ORR: Does this mean you keep away from the society of other poets as much as you can?

115

TONKS: No, I try to seek it out. At one time, of course, when I was alone, I frightfully wanted to meet other poets. Now I go and meet them occasionally as a duty but they are rather a lost set, you know, here in London. They form movements.

ORR: Do you feel, then, that contemporary poetry is a bit of a dead end?

TONKS: It could be a great deal more exciting. I don't understand why poets are quite ready to pick up trivialities, but are terrified of writing of passions. I remember it was Stendhal who was praising Byron at the time, because he said here is a great contemporary who writes of human passions, and this is something which has completely gone out of fashion, if you like. You can write if you are disgruntled, in the present day. This is quite enough to carry a poem, so current thought has it. You can have a tiff with your wife and that is enough. But all the really tremendous feelings you live by have been ignored, or people just get round them.

ORR: So the real poetry to you is a kind of elemental poetry?

TONKS: Dealing with the things which really move people. People are born, they procreate, they suffer, they are nasty to one another, they are greedy, they are terribly happy, they have changes in their fortune, and they meet other people who have effects on them, and then they die; and these thousands of dramatic things happen to them, and they happen to everybody. Everybody has to make terrible decisions or pass examinations, or fall in love, or else avoid falling in love. All these things happen and contemporary poets don't write about them. Why not?

ORR: You don't feel now that we are more conscious, say, than people were two or three hundred years ago of the world around us, the world outside us, of things which are happening in the world like starvation and (a trite thing again to say) the shadow of the hydrogen bomb?

TONKS: I think they are academically conscious of these things and that is no bad thing, because to be conscious of them at all is very important. But that is a dry consciousness. Mass starvation is an enormous theme and you need a large soul to be able to tackle it. You can't tackle it with a trivial, off-hand sensibility.

ORR: You mean you have to be able to comprehend this effect of starvation, and to feel it?

TONKS: You must feel it: otherwise how are you going to make a poem about it? It's better in prose.

ORR: And is this something that you would feel would be, for you, material for a poem?

TONKS: Well, you see, I would have to experience it. I have been to countries like India, where people are deformed and ill, and I became ill myself. It was, frankly, almost too terrible to write about.

ORR: You mean, it was too close to yourself there?

TONKS: Yes, you see, essentially, although my poems are a bit dark in spirit at the moment, I want to show people that the world is absolutely tremendous, and this is more important than making notes on even the most awful contemporary ills. One wants to raise people up, not cast them down. Or if you are going to write of these desperate things, then you must put them in their context and show the other side of the picture. This is very much a duty, isn't it?

ORR: How much of the tone of what you write depends on how you yourself are feeling at a particular moment? I mean, if you get up in the morning bad-tempered, do you write a bad-tempered poem?

TONKS: No. Because first of all, I live with the idea of the poem, think about it before I write it, and then I find the right vocabulary for it, and then I find exactly what I want to say, then I test it a hundred times with life to make sure it's true, so that it isn't thrown off quickly.

ORR: So that the writing of a single poem is a long and rigorous experience for you, is it?

TONKS: It sounds long and rigorous, but it isn't like that at all; it is frightfully exciting. All these poems have taken quite a long time, a couple of months, because there are layers of thought under them. Now I am trying to express the thought in a much lighter fashion with a colloquial comment. I am trying to develop an idea with a comment like Aristophanes. Cavafy comments also and, in fact, in the case of Cavafy the whole poem is held together by the quality of the comment, almost, which is the comment of a delightfully wryly-humoured man who has seen every kind and turn of human circumstance.

ORR: So do you feel at some point in the poem that the poet has to emerge as an editorial figure, let us say? Does he have to take sides, does he have to emerge, as one poet put it, as a bully or as a judge?

TONKS: I'm not sure about this. I don't know whether this is raising a moral question or not. Everybody who writes takes a moral decision straight away, with the very act of putting down one sentence or another, there's a moral bias to everything you write. I couldn't take up one cause especially, and I don't think I even want to stand outside my causes when I am writing about them.

ORR: Do you find yourself drawn to any particular set of themes?

TONKS: It depends. In this book, *Notes on Cafés and Bedrooms*, the themes, although different, are under the same driving force.

ORR: They're urban mainly, aren't they, with, perhaps, rural incursions, if I can put it that way?

TONKS: I'm a tremendously lyrical poet and this has had to be cut away. My poems are strongly backboned and thought out, and I would write one poem after another about nightingales and leafy grots, but I can't get a satisfactory poem out of it.

ORR: Does this mean, then, that you are very critical of your own work?

TONKS: I judge it the whole time. Only, if a poem has come off tremendously quickly, I am a bit doubtful about the language, but the actual theme of the poem has sharp scrutiny from the very first moment it enters my head, and it usually comes in after I have had conversations with people about their lives. That is what sets it off.

ORR: Do you find inspiration from *literature* in any way: not particularly poetry, drama, but, maybe, historical works?

TONKS: Oh, yes, historical stories, not historical works, which are usually so terribly badly written, because historians can't seem to learn how to write. I find French nineteenth-century literature tremendously exciting and inspiring. Once you have learnt that you can advance human sensibility in a certain way, you look at life in a new way; then you look back to literature, then you look out at life again. That's how it works, isn't it?

ORR: Have there been any writers, though, that have been a notable influence on you?

TONKS: All the great writers from Shakespeare to Chekhov, practically all French literature.

ORR: You have never found yourself writing like them and having to stop yourself consciously?

TONKS: Everybody does. The best thing about an influence is to realise it and to swallow it, and never to throw it away. It is like throwing away all the advantages of metre or rhyme, everything must be grist to your mill. You want to be on guard, but not afraid.

ORR: Somebody I was talking to in this vein recently said, 'When you say so-and-so is influenced by, let us say, Dylan Thomas, what you really mean is that he isn't sufficiently influenced by all the other writers in English literature.' Is this a point of view you would agree with?

TONKS: Yes, one always tends to find somebody who is closer to oneself than the others, or whom one admires so desperately one wants to write like him, but this can be cured. You will only find your own idiom if you are grown up. If you are a person, in addition to being a well-read person, then you can cure your reading with your life.

ORR: In fact, the main stream of inspiration is a thing or environment which is around you and pressing on you directly?

TONKS: No, which I make. Inspiration is a home-made thing. Poetry is an artificial art. The assumption that it is like dancing and singing, very close to nature, is an absolute fallacy. It is artificial from start to finish. You make it, but if it isn't based on life, however much it is praised at the time, it will die. If it works it is almost more powerful than life, in the end.

ORR: Is the sound, the physical, audible sound of your poems important to you?

TONKS: Yes, it is. But I don't think a poem is only a poem to be read. I mean to say, it has a life on the paper which is quite as good as the life it has when it is read. It does not necessarily have to be read.

ORR: But you don't feel, do you, as some of our contemporary poets do, that their poems exist really and fully on the printed page, but they don't care how they sound when they're read aloud?

TONKS: Well, you see, there is an excitement for the *eye* in a poem on the page which is completely different from the ear's reaction. Some poems, the eye can see nothing in them, literally, until they are read aloud. Basically, it would be fine if a poem could do *both*, but there are certain poems which never will do both, and are great poetry anyway.

ORR: So that you don't feel that poetry is purely and simply singing?

TONKS: No, it is not. It should do both. And, in fact, there are poems of mine which are quite difficult, but which I have put an awful lot of trouble into making musical, and the music has come over. 'Poet as Gambler', in which I laboured on the music, is difficult to read, but, in fact, it is successful, I think.

ORR: You see, when I pick up a volume of verses by someone whose verses are unknown to me, my temptation is to read them aloud to myself.

TONKS: Really? But isn't this because your ear is so well-trained that you want to test it on the part of you which is best trained to take it?

ORR: That may be so, but on the other hand, this would destroy for me the enjoyment, if I applied it all the time rigorously to every poem written for the printed page. But what I meant to ask you is, you don't have a person like me in mind when you write your poems, then, do you?

TONKS: No, I don't actually. I wish I had somebody in mind, but I feel extremely alone, I may say.

ORR: But the idea of communication, of somebody receiving, is important to you, is it?

TONKS: Yes, because one writes poems to be read, doesn't one, and there is no nonsense about that. If I make what I want to say well enough, somebody will respond to it, perhaps. I have to create my own sensibility forcefully enough for them first of all to recognise that it is valid, and also to like the sort of world I am giving them, because I am giving them a new world.

[Interview recorded in London on 22 July 1963]

FROM *The Poet Speaks: Interviews with contemporary poets by Hilary Morrish, Peter Orr, John Press and Ian Scott Kilvert*, edited by Peter Orr (Routledge & Kegan Paul, 1966) © The British Council 1966 / Estate of Rosemary Tonks 2014

Cutting the Marble

Diving into the Wreck: Poems 1971-1972 by Adrienne Rich
Studies for an Actress and Other Poems by Jean Garrigue
[*New York Review of Books*, 4 October 1973]

The first poet is very interesting. In order to understand her, we
must go into a certain room in Manhattan where a light is on over
a table. A serious woman is sitting there, writing a lesson, which is
the lesson of her life. On the paper we observe free verse stanzas
in a near-colloquial idiom with a somewhat scientific vocabulary;
they have an anonymous appearance. An occasional cockney rhyme
(sister / glamor) comes up. Reading the lines gives us the illusion,
at moments, of having gained an objective picture of events, even
of our own thoughts:

> In a bookstore on the East Side
> I read a veteran's testimony:

introduces a fact, and related materials are used to describe thought
later in the poem:

> Pieces of information, like this one
> blow onto the heap

This is well done, so that we really believe while we are reading it
that it is how thoughts behave. In this instance the idiom has
justified its impersonal quality by an ability to produce convincing
objective effects. It is the clean diction used by all good reporters
(the method of Tolstoy when he is reporting), and it is insidious
because of its invisibility. The subjective factor, with all its distor-
tions, appears to have been edited out.

What we think of *as* diction is something that brings us quickly
to the boil on an instinctive level, by throwing coloured words at
us in a way for which we are unprepared, as in the writing of
Rimbaud or of Gerard Manley Hopkins; or a rigid, thrilling block
of modern words, with a granite frost on it, which smashes us

intellectually, like a phrase of Robert Lowell's. Diction can then be identified by the autonomous life it leads; the poetry is already partly about the way it is written, and it becomes more difficult to paraphrase the content away from the page.

When a poet takes up a simpler idiom, like the one used by Adrienne Rich, subjects are of great importance. The presumption is that the poet has especially chosen a line that will allow her to cover ground of all kinds. Even so, we must be moderate in the expectations we form, for there are other difficulties in such a line – which, although fragmented, could be called a narrative line – and I shall try to show some of them. It becomes dangerous, rather than insidious, when there is insufficient fresh material within it; originally it did the work of prose and tends to be one-dimensional.

We must examine what is going on in the poems.

A cast of three or four men and women is living a life very close to the life of the newspapers; Manhattan is a living newspaper. There are refrigerators, airplanes, phone booths, hypodermics, chemicals, molecules, bombs – and subways, prisons, *rooms* where people all over the world become careworn in their efforts to face up to reality. But because these people, places, and objects are so little distinguished and personalised, we have to read minutely to assemble the essential data from which the story will begin.

There is a reason for this. The poet is careful not to impose herself on the landscape. She tries, on the contrary, to read exactly the meaning which is there, and no more, and to reproduce it without inflation. At times, a deliberately conventionalised sensibility is in fact placed so squarely before its public subject matter that we can check our emotional attitudes by it, to see whether we have them right, so to speak, as if we were checking our watches by a world clock. In the poem already quoted from, called 'Burning Oneself In', we note

the running down, for no reason
of an old woman in South Vietnam
by a U.S. Army truck

brings about the humane but unexceptional (and slightly ambiguous)

123

comment at the end of the poem:

> in bookstores, in the parks
> however we may scream we are
> suffering quietly

In Miss Rich's work, the moral proportions are valid, the protagonists are sane, responsible persons, and the themes are moving on their courses. Why is it then that we are still waiting for the poetry? At once it's obvious what has happened. She has taken on too much, and the imagination is exhausted by the effort required to familiarise itself with all the burdens of the modern world. The syntax is not there to reinvent the material, is not allowed to do so, but only to expose it. Therefore everything hangs on the uniqueness of the poet's personal contribution.

But she has almost edited herself out of the picture in the initial effort to 'get it right'. Furthermore, as we continue to read the 'narrative' line she is using, we notice that it is far more intractable than we had thought. What it can do to present facts it does very well. But once its basic character has been established in her poetry as a character of situation and event, the tone of the poetry sets hard, and it is extremely difficult to get anything else in. The line goes on quietly forcing the poet to produce more and more objective pictures in the interests of drama, tension, and news. It asks for the next action, the next scene, perhaps for the next statement – but not for the next *thought*. It would be impossible for example for an idea to be argued through to a conclusion. Similarly the lines can never have finish. It is not, regretfully we admit it, the ideal classical modern line, which can do every kind of work and for which we are searching; the one with which we can talk and think – cutting the marble with what Norman Douglas called 'the thought-laden chisel of Lysippus'.

The only way thought and feeling can be introduced at all is on the same descriptive terms as material objects. And this, as I have shown in the first quotation, is exactly what the poet has had to do. They must match in kind and degree, or the line will not tolerate them. From now on she can only think in a certain way.

The inner world that she shows us occasionally is furnished then in much the same way as the outer world; although a transfer of material objects into mental counterparts does not necessarily guarantee that we are inside, for the soul has its own landscapes. We may perhaps conclude that the basic fault of this book lies in the nature of a subject matter already familiar being joined to impersonality of presentation the result is abstraction, or politics.

Now the actual poetry in the book is elsewhere. It's entirely personal, and is to do with psychological survival. It appears out of nowhere, almost by accident:

> Nothing can be done
> but by inches. I write out my life
> hour by hour, word by word

and in another poem whose intention is hard to follow, but which is in general a series of pictures and comments on the poet's afflictions:

> You give up keeping track of anniversaries,
> you begin to write in your diaries
> more honestly than ever.

That is a personal admission which we find illuminating because it tells us something useful about ourselves. We know now that the private face that has been turned away from us is the one that can tell us things we need to know. From this snatch, we understand that the poet is rebuilding herself; the mind is still tough and fresh, even after the intellectual toil of taking on emotions not its own, as in this good descriptive piece:

> Walking Amsterdam Avenue
> I find myself in tears
> without knowing which thought
> forced water to my eyes

It goes on, 'To speak to another human / becomes a risk.' The tears are said to be evoked by a sense of outrage at certain inhuman aspects of life today, according to the poem. Tears of rage can come to our eyes in the street, but usually, if we are scrupulously truthful, from less abstract causes.

At the end of the book is a section on *The Wild Boy of Aveyron*. Psychologically, it is most revealing. Some people may have read the book by J-M Itard, or seen the film by François Truffaut, *L'Enfant Sauvage*. Briefly, a child left for dead in the woods in 18th-century France manages to survive. Some years later he is discovered, caught, and brought back into society; a human wild animal. In the film (an extraordinary film leaving an indelible impression) we are shown the child reacting to rain falling on his head, to the taste of milk, and to the safety of the forests, with their hiding places, for they alone are trustworthy.

This child is the helpless animal within every lonely alienated human creature, every poet, who from early days has found himself cut off from the minds of his fellows. He does not know how to make contact with them; his only relationship is with Nature. I suspect that it's for this reason above all others that he has entered Miss Rich's imagination.

We can see that when her intellect and her ethics have got her into a corner once again in the name of poetry, and there seems to be no way out, nevertheless she manages to write in her lesson book:

> stones on my table, carried by hand
> from scenes I trusted

This is not from the section on the wild boy; but they are certainly the stones touched, or carried, by the hand of the wild boy of Aveyron. In an attempt at wholeness the urban citizen must engross his experience within herself, for it is the part of her own story which is missing, and this is the moment in life when she needs it for her survival. In order to go back to the necessary depth, she takes the only route available from her room in the city, and makes the journey at night in her dreams:

> The most primitive part
> I go back into at night
> pushing the leathern curtain
> with naked fingers
> then
> with naked body

The regression is to an almost sub-human ancestor, frightening to consciousness, but essential to *spirit*. The day consciousness of the poet appears to stand in direct opposition to the unconscious dreamer of the night – the compensating self, who is doing all the real work, and who rights the balance by releasing buried aspects of her personality. It's no wonder that while this vital process of unification was going on the poetry regularly escaped from stanzas about current affairs. If we carelessly forget that Orpheus was especially famous for playing to wild beasts, trees, and stones, the myth which is active within us will remind us of its own accord.

Il faut être absolument moderne; but there can also be an out-of-date modernness. Early poems by Miss Rich, such as 'The Raven', 'After Dark', and 'In the Woods' (those essential woods) are more modern than many in her present book. That the contemporary nerve is wide awake in her poetry is shown in ways that pass unnoticed. For example, as we read forward we are struck by the observation that this poet never writes a love poem from which she cannot learn something useful psychologically; which forms an amusing and relevant comment on our society.

The reverse is true of Miss Garrigue, who would not have to have reasons. She would write it for its own sake.

This is her last book of poems; she died in December, 1972. We follow her into romantic territory, but we have misgivings when we observe that she has grasped the nettle – an overtly poetic manner – which has been fatal to so many other good poets before her.

Romantics (and not only romantics) tend to be lazy about first principles. By a continuous process of effort on many levels, a poem is shaken free from all that is not the poem. This is the first step, done if possible well away from a sheet of paper. It is *the* work; brutal, classical precision work to isolate, develop, and organise. Everything important is decided there and then, in order to get a poem out alive from the rapid, egocentric thought-flow of the normal mind. It's especially hard on lyric-romantic writers who have already swallowed the world and all its poets entire. Every burr sticks to their verses.

It emerges gradually that Miss Garrigue has taken up her rich, mannered style with her eyes open. There are prose stanzas in this book in which that style is dropped, and they are good. But they do not contain those lines of poetry which appear in her other verse. Her style, then, is the only way in which she can realise her potential for certain thoughts; thoughts which cannot form in the mind unless the emotional conditions are propitious to them and the clock is turned back. They cannot form in this mind and be recognised as poetry unless they resemble what has already been poetry. For she has no vision of a lyric poetry which is new is kind.

Having made these reservations, we must try to look at her work on its own terms, and there will be rewards which will make the effort worth while. With regard to other voices in her poetry, this is a good moment to remind ourselves of the continuous tradition of licensed romantic borrowing throughout history; without it, our best poets would be out of court straight away. We learn to think and feel for ourselves only by first thinking the thoughts of others, and feeling what they felt. By these means, we learn what it is to do these things.

There are some bunglers, of course. Keats, young, ill and in a hurry, lifted words and mood from the first four lines of one of the *Epodes* of Horace in order to get off the ground with 'Ode to a Nightingale' (Epode no. XIV, in Dr John Marshall's translation: 'Why 'tis that languorous sloth can thus so strongly bind / My inmost heart and mind, / As though some Lethé draught, I down parched throat had cast'). Rimbaud's '*Le Bateau Ivre*' began in stanza thirteen of '*La Bouteille à la mer*' by Alfred de Vigny. Dylan Thomas took over Edith Sitwell's territory and vocabulary. And so on. But each of these poets managed to pull a whole poem out of the pie which we recognise to be *sui generis*.

One essential aspect of Miss Garrigue's work is the presence in it of unseen forces, in the Yeatsian sense. The flowing of a mysterious charged current, especially near water or in lonely places. She is content to record it as part of her experience, interprets it pantheistically, and regards herself as part of its experience in turn. From her text it is doubtful whether she had any deeper or more exact knowledge, and she abandons mysticism the moment it no longer serves her literary purpose.

In her case this was certainly the right decision. The subject carries for most people dangerously airy-fairy overtones. Although paradoxically they also believe that this is what poetry is really about. Perhaps they dimly comprehend that human development is morally related to other words, other dimensions, which they only sense. We can only measure the importance of these strange influences by noting what happens when we are cut off from them; shut away in cities, locked into our own thoughts which harden like concrete, we become angry and ill. Whatever the case may be, they assisted Miss Garrigue to write a fine poem, 'There Is a Dark River', from an early book *The Monument Rose*. Between what is actually seen, and what is only felt, she is able to intimate an other-worldly aliveness collected under dark trees.

> There is a dark river flows under a bridge
> Making an elbowed turn where the swallows skim
> Indescribably dark in rain.

sets the scene, and although Yeats's influence is soaked into her lines here:

> Those oblivion-haunted ones who wrote
> Memorable words on the window pane,
> What but the diamond's firmness gives them name?
> And yet because they did it
> The field is thick with spirit.

due to the beauty of the expression, the poem manages to assert itself, and in the end holds its own.

In her last book she has made an effort to bring both sensibility and manner up to date; possibly she had at last woken up to the fact that her traditional poetic abilities were strangling her. The mixture is of old and new. But she begins to know herself well enough to hear her own voice. Here it is in this good opening of 'The Grand Canyon':

Where is the restaurant cat?
I am lonely under the fluorescent light
as a cook waddles in her smoky region visible through an open arch
and someone is pounding, pounding
whatever it is that is being pounded

The poem goes on to describe the canyon throughout nine extremely long stanzas. Nevertheless, there is in general a much greater variety of line treatment, much firmer ground in the way of angular, dense description. She has been forced by the subject, a wholly American subject, to write a non-European poem. There is no precedent for gathering up the whole by intuition. The material defies it in any case. Thus she is thrown back on herself and writes an original poem. As a consequence, there is only one appearance of Yeats, a mere nod, a long-legged insect (never, even for Yeats, a successful image) worked into a context entirely foreign to it in the last stanza when invention was beginning to flag. The poem softens shortly afterward and closes on a conceit; and although this is welded on to the new-look verses so that the join can hardly be seen, it has in fact nothing to do with the poem's primary conception and logic. In a natural desire to finish off by transcending gross matter, she loosens her grip and the old habits of mind reassert themselves:

under those clouds that like water lilies
enclose within them this silence received
that they graze upon and are gone.

Miss Garrigue's line always sees further possibilities in itself, and the irrelevancies it produces, which are then carefully embedded in the poems, are usually the best part. In which case they *are* the poem, and the poem is the irrelevance. Here is one of her striking images: 'the wind walked on the roof like a boy' – not factually accurate, but carrying an original concept of a wind (with more of Jean Giono than Dylan Thomas to it) to which we can assent. At the end of the same poem ('After Reading *The Country of the Pointed Firs*'), we get 'As the wind threw itself about in the bushes and shouted / And another day fresh as a cedar started.' This is aesthetically satisfying. The wind, which has been personalised, now has a life of its own. The characteristics, borrowed from a boy, are amplified and add a dimension which is valid, and the poem is refreshed and lifted out of the commonplace by them.

Still, it is unwise to base a whole method of composition on a talent for phrase-making – that is a stock-in-trade merely. Now this poet has written a number of ballads and songs, and the form of these, for the above reason, is not on her side. It rejects utterly verbal fantastification and imprecise meaning. The surface of a ballad must be as tight as a drum; it is virtually plotless, the plot is one emotion. Burns goes in deeply with 'My love is like a red red rose', and continues to refine the same emotion to the core, so that what began by touching us on a physical level ends by moving us spiritually. He makes the work easy; but it's a matter of temperament to be able to do so.

Two points should especially be mentioned with regard to Miss Garrigue's last work. In taking her step forward the poet has uncovered a gift for quick portraits:

> That man going around the corner, his pants blown out by the Wind,
> That pottering, grey-faced bakery dog,

(which comes from 'Free-Floating Report'), and for genuine insight. Although she had this in early days, it was often so badly placed that it might as well not have been there at all. The use of certain words, which inexorably draw after them other words of the same sort, obliterated it. Even now she does her best to destroy it by insipid diction, which is not the equal of the content in the following lines (from 'For Jenny and Roger'):

> Nor is their thought known to them
> Till the other give the truth away.
> They are hidden from their thought
> Till the other finds it out.

These are worth all the struggles with an overweight baggage of derivative elegies, nocturnes, laments, soliloquies, dialogues, notes, and incantations.

The Wisdom of Colette

Colette: The Difficulty of Loving by Margaret Crosland
The Thousand and One Mornings by Colette, translated by
Margaret Crosland, by David Le Vay

[*New York Review of Books*, 24 January 1974]

We call her great, for her gift to us is not limited to the art of
writing: it is the gift of a culture. I do not mean simply French
culture and taste, but that she made certain discoveries with regard
to the art of *being* which are indispensable to our lives, and which
are regularly lost in the Western part of the world.

These discoveries came about as she got round the difficulties of
her life. She became gradually the journalist of her own life, and
in that journalism are strokes of genius that befit her to receive
Nietzsche's blessing. We can think of her as the prime exemplar of
experiencing, who obtains truths which can only be got through
the agency of things. She always found life new enough not to
have to invent it; or we might put it another way, and say that
she invented it by understanding it.

Because she teaches with her life, she is, fortunately, difficult to
categorise, and belongs to philosophy as much as to literature.
Her novels, which are brilliantly written, are as novels weak. By
this I mean that when we read them we do not undergo a moral
enlargement by reason of a vision whose effects are permanent, as
we do with Tolstoy, Dostoevsky, George Eliot, or Henry James.
She did not formulate in the abstract characters powerful enough
to carry out schemes of redemption and enlightenment. That was
not her way; it might very likely have seemed to her not truthful
enough to what was all around her. And there is the danger, in
finding one's ultimate reach in literature, of losing the original
talent with which one set out. If it had cost her her seership, then
that would have been a loss so much more terrible than any gain
in re-sizing her art that it is better forgotten.

The apprehension of sensual or magical situations is her province, enveloped alive in their own detail. Her supreme moment is the Annunciation; having learned to listen, she can hear when invisible forces announce their presences in mortal things. Should this sound too abstract for rational minds, we need only remind them of the grand pattern of evolutionary and spiritual behaviour, and the humbler rhythms within the human body, and thereafter of the unseen, illogical, wholly real struggle between good and evil in the world, in order to regain their attention.

Given this basis for her writing, it will be seen that the more fresh life she lived, the stronger her work became. Life did not distract her from her thoughts; on the contrary, her *real* thoughts – the thoughts which were given to her – were outside, engrossed in life, and synonymous with it. She was never a mere clerk to her ego.

There were three marriages, a primordial mother, a daughter, a connection with the theatre as an actress and dramatist, travels, a beautician interlude, books, and success.

The irony of the story is that everything is in that first marriage to the despised Willy, the literary man about town. The first marriage made necessary, and contained, the second, which was physical. And it made possible the third, which she could have missed by not having become quite herself, and which was a natural unhasty interlocking. Willy might have been a disaster for her, but she turned the whole thing to advantage, by going along with it, and investing in it, to try to see what it meant. In his favour is the fact that he imprisoned her in the heart of the right *sort* of cloud cuckoo-land. The other dusty cages contained Proust, Anatole France, Gide, Debussy, Ravel, Satie, Schwob, Hérédia, Jarry; yesterday's broken visionaries were only just off the pavements, Baudelaire, Victor Hugo, Gautier, Mallarmé. None of this would have been so immediately possible without Willy; he educated her and appreciated her, he stood between her and the literary business-men who would have stolen her time from her as surely as he stole her books, and the money she needed to buy a life of her own.

It is worthwhile analysing how a writing style of such beauty, and capacity, came into being; and how it was underpinned by psychological growth.

In a provincial schoolroom, the schoolgirl Colette wrote a note to a friend: 'I scribbled down everything I could for her on a bit of tracing paper and launched the ball' (trans. Antonia White). If we were able to unwrap that piece of tracing paper, we would find there stubs, particles, spotlessly clean, of the idiom of *Claudine à l'école*. It's the primitive idiom of a little tomboy filled with joy and derision, whose manner of expression is kept pure by all the short cuts of laziness and illiteracy. Rimbaud's early syntax is akin to it, but more carbolic. He cuts to ribbons, jams in a stone of a word – and it sends a sheet of light at you. The pages are made insufferable, invincible, by this kind of youth. But every additional year is dangerous to it, the blows soften the mind, and Colette was about twenty-five when she wrote the first *Claudine* book.

She had read a great deal of poetry by then. Baudelaire's forest which vibrates like an organ appears two-thirds of the way through *Claudine à l'école*. She began, in general, to acquire the tone of the Symbolist poets.

The selection and treatment of descriptive detail, and the velocity of all action in this book, also suggest a reading of the masterly *Poil de Carotte* by Jules Renard, which had been published three years previously. A year before its publication, Jules Renard made a note in his diary about Colette, seen at the first night of a play with a long plait. The schoolboy *Poil de Carotte* spends most of his time at home; his quick-witted, hard-as-nails existence is aimed at us in a series of bulletins, anecdotes, and country images which are so exact that they appear harmless, when they are nothing less than implacable. A good example is the following description of a river: 'It laps with a sound of teeth chattering, and exhales a stale smell' (trans. G.W. Stonier). Colette was almost equal to this and wrote, 'Claire let off a laugh like a gas-escape' (Antonia White). She arranged her material in much the same way as Renard. Her sentencework was careful; verbs were already chosen with particular regard to the qualifying atmosphere they incorporated, their sense effect. Thus objects were 'launched', faces 'grimaced', and so on.

She was literary to the core, and her effects were calculated, as it was proper they should be. The calculation of her husband was of a different order when he asked her to put in 'some patois, lots of local words, some naughtiness, you see what I mean?' Nevertheless, without his original suggestion, his conception of the book that might emerge if she set down some of her school memories, there would have been no book. He first had the idea of writing it himself, after lunching at her old school. Then in addition, without his efforts to make it scandalous, it would never have had the enormous worldly success which it had. Finally, he 'arranged all the propaganda he could by all the means he could possibly think of'; he was a very great literary agent. As is well known, he published the book under his own name; having called it into being, he stole it away from Colette.

Margaret Crosland tells us that Colette's signature was added to the contract with Willy's; a significant fact. Colette knew, and her friends knew, who had written *Claudine à l'école*.

The deep psychological benefit to Colette of what followed must have been extraordinary. From that moment no matter what happened, underground, in the darkness, the place of fear and trembling, the gain had been registered – and that is where life truly begins. Despite an everyday existence of unchanged and indifferent quality, everything suddenly became possible, it came within reach. In the material world, it is extremely useful to become lucky before you can become unlucky. Your contemporaries get into the habit of liking you: and you are able to retain your daring.

Colette could not do anything about her success. She appears to have been a very young twenty-seven, with slight grasp of externals. She was in any case separated from reality by Willy. Evidently she found it extremely hard to credit things for what they were; she stuck fast, dreaming out her dream – and writing it down. In this condition she produced further *Claudine* books for Willy, and *silently took an immense step forward*. Her writing started to be very good. Twentieth-century Paris read her refreshing pages, pages of light temper, witty and clean-running; Willy, the taskmaster, struck in certain musicianly comments, and the books were all equally successful.

The drama behind her silent progression had been as follows. Her childish idea of herself had run on unchecked after marriage, and Willy had fostered it; in fact it was *all she had*. Suddenly she found out that he was unfaithful. The shock to her ego was more than it could bear; there was nothing inside capable of withstanding the blow, her personality was fragmented, and she collapsed into a nervous breakdown. At that moment she lost her childhood, and no longer knew who she was. Sido, her mother, came to Paris to nurse her, and helped her to pick up the thread of her own story again – and this is the very thread by which life hangs. When it was all over, and as soon as she began to write the first *Claudine*, she found herself, and could repair her identity. But this time a new self was in charge. It prescribed physical exercises for her body, and undertook the task of learning how to think, and *be*; the spirit stopped still and listened – an Oriental skill.

This mature work went on for eight years. From twenty-five until she was thirty-three, her thoughts wrote thoughtful letters to themselves. The mind restocked itself with itself. There was eventually so much life inside that she began mentally to live without her husband. And at the end of that time she had enough strength to move away from him *physically*. She had formed herself, and woken up. She was also capable of being alone if it was necessary.

Knowing how to be alone is a part of the wisdom of wild animals. Colette had never broken her bond with nature, and this includes the inanimate. The secret is commitment, detail, and alertness. Nature mystics would explain that you make friends with what is there; an animal, a plant, an object. Colette possessed herself of this knowledge and used it consciously throughout her life and in all her writings. Thus she arrived at the end of her time with Willy with a certain incomprehensible strength, and he was anxious to be rid of her.

Colette emerged as Pierrette, and with Willy's help went on the stage. In the first book published as her own while still married, she wrote, 'I mean to go on dancing in the theatre.' It was called

Dialogues de bêtes, a new genre. There was a rapport with Rudyard Kipling. The idea of animal conversations came most probably from his stories (which she mentions in *Claudine à l'école*), with their nicknames which described the characteristics of the animals, Stickly-Prickly and Bi-Coloured-Pythons-Rock-Snake.

The next development is profoundly instructive. Colette took her animals on the stage with her. She acted out of herself certain creatures, pure instincts, which had been locked up in a den inside for thirteen years. She personalised the animals of her subconscious, and *drew its sting*. All her natural desires, all her rage, instead of eating her internally – and one thinks of the expression 'eating her heart out' – ceased to be harmful to her.

Becoming what she was in deeper levels of her mind brought about a physiological renewal. Her flesh was transformed by her psyche's good health. Albert Flament described her later in life, for the process continued, 'luscious arms – combing rapidly her short, thick hair, surrounding herself with a chestnut foam.... Eyes *made* for the stage, slanting upwards, and between their thick lashes, a look of youth, of *joie de vivre*, a spark of light so brilliant that it looks artificial....'

The years from thirty-three were those of the great test of strength. 'Missy', the Marquise de Belboeuf, was photographed standing with protective kindness behind Colette; one observes a somewhat sloping coastline, silk dressing-gown lapels, and the face of a manly, strong-minded nanny rabbit. Exactly what was needed. Colette was now playing George Sand, succubus and incubus, and although she would get into bed with Missy, she does not appear ever to have been deeply in love with a woman, which is an entirely different matter. She and Missy amused themselves immensely, and started scandals effective enough for fresh waves of publicity.

Colette continued her journalism, and contributed to *Le Matin*. In 1911 this great reporter and *pierrette* published *La Vagabonde*. It was a triumph. The book proceeds by scenes, dramatic reveries, and letters to plot through a love affair, nothing more, and in this case that is nothing less than everything. Motives and scruples are scanned familiarly by the inner eye. The quality of the sensibility is a lesson in itself; the needle quivers under the slightest vibration. Here is the parting between the heroine, Renée Néré, and her lover, Max. (Fossette is Renée's dog.)

> Fossette has squeezed between us her bronze-like skull, which gleams like rosewood....
> 'Max, she's very fond of you; you'll look after her?'
> There now, the mere fact of bending together over this anxious little creature makes our tears overflow.
>
> (trans. Enid McLeod)

It is the homeliness and exactitude of the emotion that tells. It comes from a real life, cannot be got anywhere else, and is as fine as George Eliot's humble drawn-thread work.

The following year Sido died. Colette lost so much of herself with this death that she spent the rest of her life writing about her. A second fundamental change took place. The spirit changes its condition of being, so to speak, it perceives there is another kind of life. After the baptism by death, Colette the wise woman was born, a person in authority.

She married Henri de Jouvenel three months later, and had a daughter by him. She had earned her daughter, and she could afford, psychologically and financially, to make this mistake. In any case it was irresistible, and had to be. Each side misconceived the other, and recovered from previously prepared positions, but slowly, going into years.

Chéri was published when Colette was forty-seven; and was said to be her masterpiece. It contains scenes which are of an emotional and aesthetic perfection; the marriage of symbolism and sexual experience. Yet it is static, even cold. In a large measure this is due to the central character, Chéri, who is perhaps a representation of an elemental, or nature spirit; he is two-dimensional and has no inner life. He comes from myth, from *The Tempest*, and all serious fairy stories. He is real enough, and can be described, like fire or water, but he will not go successfully into the fabric of human relationships which constitutes a novel. Placed at the centre of a story, he petrifies the humanity, neutralises the action, and renders all moral operation irrelevant. He is an essence and is imponderable. As a concept in himself, Colette knew she had made an important discovery. What she did not realise was that the nonhuman aspects of her subject were affecting her. The aesthetician predominates and repeats herself more often in this book than in any other, as though afraid to change the imagery that furnishes it, and only daring to rechisel. There are even moments when she thinks with words; low water for so great a writer.

Many novels, stories, autobiographical writings, and occasional pieces followed on; the articles for *Le Matin* are only now available in English (*The Thousand and One Mornings*). When at last Colette married Maurice Goudeket the foundations were solid, and from her happiness a flow of practical information comes to us; it is hard news. Her daily life has been converted by her into a raw material. She reports on it, as though she is a foreigner there. Now it can happen that between the reporter and the scene reported something is transmitted – and if it is written down immediately an uncanny electric truth is obtained. Normally this is only achieved by writing fast; or by being written by the facts. Colette was able to take on the wing such a revelation by mercury. It may be found in the atmosphere of the whole piece, its "entity", or in half a sentence which brings our whole lives into focus. To paraphrase some words from the Koran, she says what she does not know. It is the quality that lifts her work into another class – another degree, the degree of master novelists, philosophers, mystics, and other grand masons of human development.

Margaret Crosland's new interpretation of Colette is required reading for the Hamlets of London and New York. It is as good as her first study, *Madame Colette*. She has rethought her subject, added new facts, and filled in the Missy period between the first two marriages, and the early days with de Jouvenel. Willy emerges even more sympathetically. The book should be read on the spot, drained down to the dregs in one glance, bibliography, dates, italics, photographs, everything.

The Pick-up or L'Ercole d'Oro

There will be hot-house winds to blunt themselves
Against the wooden bathing-huts, and fall down senseless;
Lilos that swivel in the shallow, iced waves, half-submerged;
Skiffs – trying to bite into a sea that's watertight!

IN SEPTEMBER the warm sea slows down. How long the pauses are
... then it starts up, first to the left, then far down to the right.
Shallow waves pour themselves uphill in a lemonade jelly.

A huge purple headland, with its roads and trees blotted out by
the heat, is fitted weightlessly along the top of the water. Just near
it, a boat seems to navigate for an eternity across the transparent
mass on which it balances.

You hear the drone of an antique seaplane toiling up around the
curve of the earth.

Some German tourists are swimming about in the bay. They
wear hats, and their bone-dry heads stick up out of the water. As
it moves, each seafaring head pulls along behind it sparkling wet
folds of liquid. They talk to one another with a sharp noise like
ducks quacking. Far below them in deep emerald water their limbs
float down.

A local boy gets up out of this huge bath, and walks ashore. He's
wringing wet, with the drops running off his nose, and a saturated
pad of hair stuck down around his features. He throws himself to
the ground, and hugs the beach to him. It's hotter than a human
body, as hot as a cake from an oven. The breeze blows a wave of
fire over his flesh.

Up at Bar Mimi, lunch has begun. Bathers move along the low
whitewashed walls to find themselves wooden tables. There's a roof
of cane thatch overhead, as grey as driftwood.

In the shade up there, everyone's alive. Two boys run about
taking orders and writing them down in a blue sloping script with
a *penna stilografica*. Bottles of yellow wine are brought, two at a
time; held by the necks, they clink.

That woman quite alone, the old one, is the Signora Danielli. She's properly dressed-up for lunch at home, and no one knows what she's doing here where everyone else is young, naked, and burnt. She's brought with her a certain authority, and this being so, after a while it seems quite natural that she should be here. She takes such an interest in everything that goes on that she makes herself part of it, and looks about with her pleasant oldish face and speaks good Tuscan Italian. People soon get used to her, and even nod and say respectfully, *'Buon giorno. Signora'* as they pass her table. After a quarter of an hour, she's almost invisible.

Now there are two tables right at the front, facing the sea, which interest her very much. Something is going on there. At first she only glances at them from time to time, but in the last few minutes she's had the impression that things are speeding up, and she feels that at her age she can't afford to miss a second of it.

At the table on the left, a pretty young woman and an older woman in sunglasses are eating a chicken dish. They don't talk to one another, because the young woman feeds herself and her cocker spaniel, and the older one does nothing but talk to a man at the next table.

This man is at first sight nothing special. A sturdy fellow, about thirty-four years old, he's dressed in a new white American T-shirt with a circular machine-sewn badge on the chest, showing a crown above two fish-like shapes. Out of the T-shirt come red bronze forearms, a massive neck, and on top the face of a handsome char. He could be Italian, but there's not enough black in the features for a Procidian, and if he was a Neapolitan there would be those plump cheeks which droop. No: that handsome woman's face has a red-brown varnish, that's all wrong, and so are those scrupulous fingernails. The grain of his skin is so fine it looks as though it has been scoured clean by a high wind full of salt. Auburn hair, bobbed to show how thick it is, goes down to just below his ears.

An engineer, hydraulic engineering, from the Balkan states. Or a gymnast. One senses that in some way his profession is connected with water; it can be read in the tone of his flesh and in the exceptional cleanness of his whole person. He sits lightly, as very fit people do who no longer feel the weight of their bodies.

He and the older woman have so much in common, their voices flow together. He has the mannerism of following his thoughts along with his eyes, so that he seems not to look at anything in particular, but to focus inwardly like an old-fashioned intellectual. Another surprise – he has meticulous good manners. His eating and drinking are done with the minimum of fuss. How curious to observe so much style in what is clearly an invincible body.

THE MANNERS of the pretty young woman couldn't be worse. They're revolting. She's dressed as if she's just got up; a lilac robe with the hood thrown back. It's fastened deep down in the bosom, like a seductive dressing-gown, has trumpet sleeves and an embroidery of lilac beading on the shoulders. The colour suits her perfectly. On her brown plump throat is a chain with a shiny coin which swings and catches in the V of her wrap each time she leans backwards. Her hair is untidy; it's drab-dark with locks of white lamb's wool run through it in the current Italian fashion. She's about twenty, a woman of the world, and her small pretty arms with their white undersides play about all the time.

At this moment her fork is pointed to the heavens with a dripping hot piece of chicken skewered on it. She picks off the meat with her fingers, and dangles it over her dog. Then she laughs loudly and feeds the lump straight down into its jaws. No sooner done than she's back at her plate, getting another forkful for herself this time, and chewing it over enjoyably. And so it goes on; without a glance for anyone, she eats and drinks, wiping off her mouth on her knuckles and throwing bones on the ground, as though she was entirely alone there, and in any case didn't care a fig for anyone.

The older woman with the sunglasses is not unattractive. And with another low concentrated sentence the burnished man attends on her. He seems to need to browse over her face for the rights and wrongs of his argument.

She wants to smoke.

He's up like a monkey. That awkward gritty noise is an old flint lighter – and look at the protective brick wall he's made, it's like a fortress built over her. Off to his own table again, his sex controlled to the teeth. He tosses his head and drops back into the discussion exactly where they left it. He nags her on, they catch fire just as before, and burn furiously.

What on earth makes people talk away like that? Signora Danielli turns her ear, trying to get a few words into it... car insurance, yes of course, it's compulsory throughout Italy now, everyone knows about it. But is that really a good enough reason for him to frown, to look as deep as a dagger into himself, and to vibrate with emotion, all at the same time?... The ferry out of Naples on a rough day, and they *will* load on lorries of ten thousand kilos, when lorries over five thousand kilos are strictly forbidden. Sunglasses has suffered on account of the lorries, and the way the ferry lurches – both the talkers lurch as the ferry strikes the high seas. Well, says the burnished man, that is the fault of the syndicate; they run everything. Be philosophical! He's counselling her, with a hand in repose on each of his elastic knee-caps. He's content so long as he's free to live an uncomplicated open-air life. As an innocent low-brow, he takes a great breath of it on the spot – oh, what it must be like, what torture, to be enclosed indoors in a terrible box filled with stale air. Sunglasses has to admit that she, too, gets choked by the staleness of the air indoors. He's so satisfied by her answer, and finds her whole personality so congenial to him, that he swings his head off to the side as though he wants to relish the reply and have it to himself for a second longer. By chance this movement takes in the back view of a well-built German girl in a bikini who has just that second got up from the table behind and is now buying herself a Coca-Cola at the bar.

Sunglasses also finds that she can be choked by a bedroom full of stale air at night. He's even more delighted, and sweeps his head off in another pleasurable movement, as the German girl returns and so can now be seen from the front.

Isn't there something masculine about the way Sunglasses goes at her cigarettes? Possibly that is what makes him feel at ease. She's so freedom-loving, a bold comrade, and as stylish as he is, puffing away there, and even swinging her head good-naturedly, to chew things over, as he does. She appears somehow to draw attention to some feminine aspects of the burnished man: too much quivering along the mouth line, it's so womanish to change it every second like that, for what would happen in a crisis? But still the tremendous flow of energy he's directing towards the table of the two women (and it never slackens), *that* is overwhelmingly masculine.

THERE ARE TWO OTHER CHAIRS at their table, and a wicker bag on each. What a bad arrangement, for if one of the chairs was empty, why, the comrades could sit together and smoke together in harmony. Sunglasses is aware of this, and she hesitates for an instant with her arm raised – if she clears the chair beside herself, won't it seem as though she is inviting him to sit rather close? And that would be too obvious and might repel him and drive him off. Whereas if she clears the chair farther away, she is stating plainly that – that she needs the bag which is lying on it.

The curious part of it is that as she takes hold of the bag, both the lilac girl and the burnished man look away involuntarily, as if it was something they should not have seen.

Now that the set has been cleared, Signora Danielli looks at her watch; she behaves like a good director who has acted in many of her own films, and murmurs: *'Trenta secondi.'*

Thirty seconds. And the burnished man gives the impression that he has all day. He seems to slow down. Ah, he's bored, he's lost interest; he's *stopped talking* altogether.

Outside, over his shoulder, you can see that a launch has approached with an engine whose beat is buried in water. Driven by a man in white, it hangs from the beach by the nose, wallowing as the sea moves it from side to side, while it continues to throb.

There's a hiss – one of the waiters levers the metal cap off a bottle. It flies away and hits the ground under the legs of a spotted dog which is roaming there, and which starts back.

The burnished man is ready to leave. It's all at an end. He stands up, and takes a step forward, looking for a boy to bring his bill. No one comes, so he's forced to sit down again just before leaving – he sits down therefore in the nearest chair, which is now the one from which the bag was taken. He seems to be put out – no one likes waiting for a bill – and not entirely aware of what he is doing, because he takes a piece of bread from the bread basket as though he were still alone at his own table, filling in time. He ignores the women, frowns as usual, and goes on concentrating – on what? On his own thoughts, which have always interested him so much. Grudgingly he admits by his gestures that there are, after all, other people at the table with him. They must have moved in to his table when he got up to leave a moment ago. In any case, it is *his* table, it always has been, but courteously he offers both the women some bread from his basket so that they don't feet uneasy.

THE BURNISHED MAN begins to talk. This time he speaks only to the lilac girl, to whom he has not previously said one word. His voice is pitched deeper. He is less of a philosopher, much less fond of the open air than he was. Sunglasses listens with interest, and waits patiently for her turn in the conversation, but it does not come. She wants to smoke; then let her smoke! No one is going to stop her. She sits where she has always sat, and although a minute or two ago she had a companion at her table and someone to talk to at the next, she now has two complete strangers, unknown persons, who ignore her and speak only to one another so rapidly that it becomes a dialect no one else can understand.

How frightful to be brushed off like that as if one was lower than the dirt. The most hardened would be sapped and dispirited. She's so low that if they were to give her one word, she could make a meal out of it, and pull herself up and move her limbs a little. It's so exhausting putting up a fight alone, the joints become rigid and fasten the body together in one position and there's no juice to unfasten it.

They will not rescue her, because they have forgotten she is there. If she was to draw attention to herself, they would then see her, and might possibly speak to her: who knows?

Presently she makes a fierce effort: she rises to her feet and pushes back her chair. To her, it's like a bomb exploding. But no one has heard the sound. She sways, nearly off balance, and with her beach-bag walks away carefully. As though she has a scar on her face, she cannot quite manage her features, the shock seems to have given them a wrenching. But the further she removes herself from the two brutal young bodies at the table, the greater is her well-being.

She gets herself down to the beach. On the burning white sands she spreads an orange towel, and prepares herself for a sunbath and a siesta. Quite worn out by life, she drops off into unrefreshing middle-aged slumbers. As the ugliness leaves her face, it turns into one of those curious death masks which are taken from a musician or a poet who has been defeated by life and resurrected by death; smooth, peaceful faces, they become perfect examples of other-worldliness, and thus the noble face of Death itself.

And *they*? Signora Danielli watches them.

They talk with hunger and thirst; with a radiant thoughtlessness. Their bodies, already prepared by water and fire for such a meeting, sense the approaching moment of supreme carnal gratification. Beside this, nothing else matters.

They talk until they've talked themselves out. And then, each golden barbarian rests, with eyes passively turned away from the other, the feast to come. You don't look directly when you want something as much as that. They appear expressionless... almost idiotic... but above all, monstrous.

WHO IS GOING to pay the bill for this interesting lunch? On the island the young males who stand at street corners and stare with onyx eyes, hissing like snakes at foreign women who attract them, expect to be paid for and to receive presents.

The lilac girl rummages and finds one of those flat leather purses which are made in North Africa and sold around the Mediter-ranean to tourists by itinerant Genoese. It's closed by a fringed

146

flap which tucks into a slot, and is decorated on the back by two brightly coloured strips of leather threaded through the glaciated manilla surface. Ridiculous object! You couldn't get anything into it – not even a wad of Italian money, the coloured paper rags they use. She opens it, looks inside, gives a pretty trill like a handbell being rung, closes it and stows it away again. Out comes a buckle made of imitation stones – some dress-making project: she holds it in dimpled hands with little fingers which fasten and unfasten themselves as children's do.

So the meal is over. Up they get, smiling pleasantly at one another like strangers again, and casually, without a backward glance, they separate. The lilac girl with her spaniel, her untidy bag, her looped robe, passes the table of Signora Danielli.... Oh, that voluptuous cold puppy fat on her little face, how rich. And the cork sandals that slip off her heels, they're so sluttish, so high and silly, she can hardly walk in them. She turns towards the beach and joins the figure which is drowning in sleep on the orange towel.

The burnished man pays his bill matter-of-factly, as though he always spends exactly that amount. The boy doesn't ask him about the bottles or total up a long list, so it's clear he pays for no one but himself. While he does it, that thick back is toward the beach. He won't look at her, won't look at the lilac wrap coming off. He's devoted to his pockets, his wallet, and carefully buttons away some money into his shorts, and makes it neat. Having got together his personality in this way, he's ready for his car and strolls out. There's something so grim and fixed about his eyes... in his head, among all those thoughts, is he holding intact some essential datum which were chattered out piecemeal across the tablecloth? 'No. I hate Bar Elio, it's full of old, old men ugh! Our road's so nice, and the house, who wants to go out and be goggled at by old men? The rose-coloured house in the Via Baiola. I'm always there in the evenings, lazing about.' What a vapid, futile little mind; he would have pounced on the words, and from that moment was dead to the world.

Signora Danielli notes that his is the yellow Alfa Romeo with

147

the hood down. The tyres jerk and throw back sandy dust. From zero the machine vanishes down the road, whining, and that's the last of him.

The Signora catches herself stretching after the entertainment. The boys are rolling up tablecloths filled with breadcrumbs; there's a pile of plates, greasy forks stick out of them. Oh it's quite finished.

She knows what she's seen; a piece of her own youth. That reckless piece, it trapped her, and made her live a certain kind of life, not the kind she wanted at all. To think that she'd forgotten what it felt like, the elemental sex happiness which belongs to the animal kingdom, and which makes you behave so badly. Five tables away she's seen it all again, hideous idiot joy, in which the actors are lost and mad, and their poor accomplices become the same.

She's so sorry for them. And grateful to think that she doesn't have to wash and get ready for a lover.

Yes, she's old, but wide awake. When she escaped from that sort of youth, she got away only by ageing, only that way did she obtain real life. And now she walks in the marble of her library; her etched features look inward and outward; she has arrived at herself. That is the classical Italian happiness; the great joy and gaiety of understanding yourself.

THE SUN REACHES the waters of the horizon at seven o'clock and at once goes out. Sometimes a cloud left over from the day maintains a red flame on board for half an hour into the night. Sweet water dews fall silently down the mountain slopes.

Primitive peoples go to bed early, for everyone fears the dark.

A wind gets up on one side of the island... under cliffs of un-polished marble, there's a piling up of waves, a moaning that begins in the telegraph wires.

Here's Signora Danielli. She's parked her car and now steps back in the dirt road to look up into infinity at the Milky Way, the *Via Lattea*, of which she is a part.

By the light of it, she can also see that her two cats are watching her attentively from the driveway of her house. They run off as she approaches, and leave a dark object on the ground.

She has her husband's stick in her hand; the object may be an animal. Close to, she can see it's a large rat, a dark piece of instinctive life force, which they've killed and brought for her. She's turning it over gently with the stick, and it rolls softly in two sections like chamois bags of trinkets, when there's a blast, enough to split her eardrums, and a blinding light flashes on and off high up the mountain. Every stone shakes in its socket, and the vibration runs through her body. A storm has begun.

At that moment the rat comes to life. Ignited by the shock, it leaps gracefully into the air like a dancer, with the tips of its delicate feet hanging beneath it. Signora Danielli says compassionately: 'Poor thing, poor thing. I must kill it.' She strikes it feebly with her stick, so that it jumps up again and again, in a reflex action, each time higher than the last. And frisks about on the tips of prehensile bones in a spirited way, while the clouds grumble like a barracks full of soldiers and shoot out crackling shots.

She has to hit, hit, hit. When it's over, she's panting and trembling. She leans on the stick, still watching it with fierce eyes, for a long time.

WHEN SHE GOES inside she feels so uneasy that she stops to breathe in the familiar smell of the hall, but she seems to have brought in with her the wet darkness from outside, and the sickly wind that was blowing in the garden. Overhead, two gigantic air-shapes with sheer sides of rock, collide, trying to split one another open. You can hear the blistering and cracking of the seams.

She mounts the staircase to her bedroom.

There's a light on in her husband's large dressing-room next door. This is the irritating, beloved husband who made her change her life so many years ago. He's moving about on some business of his own, according to a set of thoughts which are entirely unknown to her.

Oh but the thunder! Now it bears down solely on the house in an effort to smash the roof in; the electric light bulbs flicker. At

149

any moment there may be total darkness: the island's supply is always confused by an electric storm.

Her husband is pulling drawers open impatiently in the old *armadio*... the thunder shifts its position, and a watery cough goes off far into the distance, echoing as it strikes against unseen obstacles and passes through great empty rooms, through the august *Sala di Giove*, and on and on... then she can hear the domestic sounds of the bouse again, and the double rap of the drawer handles as they fall back on the wood, rat-tat. He's looking for something: possibly he's going out for the evening? She cheers up at once. She won't be expected to cook dinner; she can go to her books. She can spend the evening quietly finding out the attribution of 'Ayin' among certain old volumes with end-papers of marbled plum. The pleasure of it floods over her in a rush of blood as sweet as honey.

He *is* going out. She remembers now; she told him he was driving too fast, and he opened the lid of his eye at the corner and showed her some light green crocodile water. How furious he was! He let her see what was going on inside, but he had no idea of *how much* he'd shown her. He lowered the lid, after he'd given her a sight of the green water, and they walked along together, side by side, thinking it over. She was very interested by what she had seen. He would have to be teased; or, if he wouldn't respond to that, then he would have to be fought with. She could never afford to relax, since he shifted his ground psychologically every minute. If she became intimidated, she would go under forever. 'It took me twenty years to learn how to be rude to you,' she would think, looking at him, 'and you *like* it. But I do not.' 'When he goes out,' she thinks later, 'I must remember to be sharp to him, as though I have a grievance. That kiss on his neck, behind the ear, the one that keeps him sealed in and made safe by my love while he's out in the world, that must go... or I shall lose value in his eyes.'

AN OLD MAN of sixty-eight opens the door of the dressing room, and stands there, fastening a despatch case. He has a handsome toast-dry face, peevishness gives it life. He wants to be prevented from doing what he is doing, and from leaving the house in the middle of a storm in his well-pressed grey suit with the brown silk handkerchief tucked in the pocket.

Out of habit, she opens her mouth spontaneously to tell him about the rat; then stops herself. She hasn't worked over the story to see whether it does her credit; if there's a weak spot he'll use it against her. She becomes her husband for an instant and passes the thing through his mind.

Although she hasn't said a word, the old man has seen her lips move. He at once hastens off downstairs, convinced that she's going to intercept him, which is exactly what he wants. In the hall, he struggles into his coat with the thought that he's being nagged to death, and flies out into the darkness as the first drops of rain fall. He's punishing her by leaving her alone in the middle of a storm. For his part, he's from a very old Neapolitan family, and the storms of the Mediterranean are in his blood. They invigorate him with what he is already; he's more decisive, flashing, aristo-cratic, at these times when the ordinary people bury themselves in the ground, or in their houses, with their wet dogs clinging to them and belly-crawling on the floor beside them. For the same reason he drives his car fast, and be will not be shackled and reduced to an impotent booby, when such boldness is his by right of birth.

She listens calmly to the steps of this man so stuffed with insolent bad behaviour. He will have reached the eucalyptus trees by now, and will be opening the door of the car. Because he is alone, he will drive very carefully and quite slowly after all. He will go straight to Tonino's; no, to Marcello's, in the port. And they will all turn towards him and light up as he comes in, since he's known to be a born story-teller. He'll sit down, make the 'thump' on the cloth with his closed fingers which is the prelude, and begin to be amusing. It only takes a minute or two, and people go red and their eyes shine with stupid glee. Women, underwear, lavatories, husbands, these subjects are well known to be funny in the first place, but if you cram them into an Italian meat mincer all over again, out come brand new sausage jokes, naked, obscene, childish. It's appalling to have a quick and filthy mind like that, to wink, and raise your little old man's finger in the air and wag it about.

They say he could go on the stage, and get paid for it. But he prefers to be close to people, and laughs along with them and goes a good dark red himself. In no time they're all roasting hot, it's like a volcano in there, they bang on the tables and yell: *'Basta!'* He dries his face – which is streaming – and grows younger every minute. You can just see the sort of young man he used to be... there, *now*, there's the *Ercole d'Oro*, see the way he breathes in contemptuously in a long-drawn-out sneer? He was once a glowing, lustful fellow with a great black chin with an oily dent in it: the women must have gobbled him up. But then, why the story-telling? To keep the cold out, of course. Otherwise old age would get inside and creeping death would reach the viscera, especially the liver. He needs the heat of other healthy human beings constantly, in order to remain alive. But he must have a reason for waylaying them, and getting them to sit down and unbutton their coats... .

And so this handsome well-dressed man becomes a joke-jobber. When the fire goes out of him, as it does regularly, in fact nearly every day, he drives off, off, away from his house with its books and sofas and the polished chequerboard floors where his wife walks about.

'Vitti, Vitti, have I done this?' Signora Danielli asks the man in her head. She's lighting an oil lamp and bends over it.

Immediately the house is engrossed in the darkness of the mountain: the electricity has failed on this side of the island.

She now has a circle of yellow light, and goes and comes within it, bringing kitchen candles to be lighted. This primitive task reassures her, and as each flame develops and burns steadily, her thoughts settle.

The rattling noises of the branches against the walls, and the sea wind that stops the rain hissing into the ground and carries it off sideways with a dolorous moan... these things are necessary so that the grave Italian interior may double its peace. Nothing moves. The table where the lamp stands is the centre of the world. To sit still there is to be in touch with everyone and everything. How the books along the walls excite her; the titles are serious and contain real knowledge, they are always new because each time you read them the same words say something different. There are works by Maxwell on the Tarot, on Alchemy, on Persian seers, on Sai Baba. In this earthly paradise, she cuts with a little alabaster paper-knife into the cartridge paper of a new book; rough edges form. She has entirely forgotten her husband's existence.

PRESENTLY — it's as though someone has called to her — she lifts her head and listens intently... some ineffable matter....

They will be meeting about now, the burnished man and the lilac girl. He'll go to her house after dinner; it's all arranged, and they can't wait any longer. Sunglasses will have to go up to her room; it'll be one of those small white-washed rooms with damp marks low down, with an icon painted as though by a child, and an unsteady wicker table. She'll be sent up to her room after she's played bath-attendant. For the lilac girl will soak herself slowly, and call out from her bath often; the spaniel will walk in and out of the open bathroom door while she splashes water at it. When she steps out, so slippery, to dry herself, Sunglasses will put the cigarette into her mouth as she hands her that expensive rough towel, which she'll tuck under her armpits. And lifting up her arm to get it right, she will look into the hollow of her young armpit, as white as a groin.

When the lights go out, the lilac girl will go on drying herself in the warm darkness; she'll be able to see perfectly well. And she'll scoff at her dog because it whimpers and is craven.

Then Sunglasses will bring a lighted lamp through the night to this indoor bathing scene, and the girl will already be dressed in her lilac robe. Her body will already smell of Calèche, that heavy Parisian powder which is for much older women, because it dresses the skin with the milky dust of another skin as heavy as soil, and makes it plump. As for her hair, she'll have pushed it up in tresses on top of her head; she can't be bothered to do it. The atmosphere of the lamplight allows one to be slack. But for the shuddering behaviour of her dog, she would be ideally contented in these conditions. Accustomed to making a slow toilet, in any circumstances whatsoever, she's at home on the earth. With Arab-style gestures that concentrate the whole mind, she brings the cosmetics she wants within her circle of movement. Her arms bend and stretch themselves forth; it's impossible to look away from her.

And when the knocking on the door comes, in the middle of the storm – a man like that will always arrive in the teeth of fire and water – it will be Sunglasses who has been listening for it, who raises her eyebrows dreadfully, and leers: 'The Devil is here!' It will be the lilac girl who ignores it, and goes on brushing with her hairbrush the warm flesh of her dog's silky ear. And keeps her eyes turned away.

Sunglasses will go upstairs because they are stronger than she is; the force of it is too much for her.

Only when she's closed the door of her room, only then will the lilac girl stir herself. On her way to the front door, she'll stoop and pat her spaniel on the head.

THEY SAY that the helicopter station is the ugliest spot on the island. It consists of a square of concrete which juts into the sea and has a blockhouse on one corner.

Signora Danielli is waiting for her husband who has gone to Naples for the day. She's under a poor-looking tree, just a scraggy thing frizzed up by the hot concrete. There are cars parked along the roadside, and in one of them, lo and behold, the lilac girl alone with her dog.

The helicopter flies in badly, like a hornet. It luffs and is unsteady. A boiling wind, full of grit, buffets the Signora. Her skirt whips itself against her legs, her hair tugs away from her head, and she holds to the tree for support.

The machine comes to rest, screaming, tipped about on three

soft legs. While the blades of the propeller go on thudding round horizontally, steps are wheeled up to a door which opens underneath it, and people start to get out with hasty movements like marionettes.

She can see her husband bending down inside at a window, and waves to encourage him. The lilac girl is out of the car and waving also. Signora Danielli looks for the burnished man. In conventional clothes, he must definitely be a god... but no sign of him.

Then it must be Sunglasses she's meeting. But no, she's not there either.

Then it is some entirely unknown person.

A middle-aged man carrying a despatch case and an umbrella hurries forward and embraces the lilac girl. He is bald, with glasses, and quite short; a strong pale nose sticks out. He's rich, obviously; everything about him appears to be new. Only he himself is a little worn, with lines and thoughts, against the worsted cloth, the crocodile and gold that show here and there. He holds her to him, deep feeling binds them; he loves her, and is besotted with her.

As for the lilac girl, it's a metamorphosis. Those animal gestures of the worldly-wise concubine which Signora Danielli thought belonged to her, those atrocious manners and hidden eyes – they're gone in a puff of smoke.

A happy schoolgirl looks straight into the eyes of her only friend and laughs out loud with joy. The lilac girl rubs her head against his coat, and can't stop talking for one minute.

He gets into the driving seat of the car and pulls gently at the ear of the dog, which tries to climb into his lap.

With the animated lilac girl beside him, he starts the engine. How happy they are; he drives, and laughs, without taking his eyes off the traffic.

'Vitti, *cara*. It's been a good day, I can see that. No, you don't look tired, not at all. Here? Well, nothing very much. I had to get Filippo to tie up the creeper, it was broken by the storm. And we buried the rat, so you won't trip over it again.'

She knows from his expression that it has not been a good day.

155

There is the first sad glance from the *via dolorosa* of his thoughts. Oh, how disappointed he always is. And she tries to give him everything, to renew everything for him, so that life will be good enough for him. But he turns away, ill with nerves; he can't bear it when she beseeches him to be happy, against his will. And is so happy herself, for no particular reason.

They walk to their car, side by side, in silence.

She gets a sight, in the distance, of the other car just disappearing. The car she might have been in forty years ago. if she'd married her friend. But instead she married her lover. And that road led her only to herself.

'All because of a certain feeling he gave me, once or twice, which made me cry out, *'Now I shall not have lived in vain!'* Because I expected that feeling from life, and tried to take it for myself, it promptly vanished. And now I can't even remember what it was like. And don't even care.'

This short story was originally published in *Encounter*, XL no.1 (January 1973). The epigraph is the third stanza of 'The Ice-cream Boom Towns' (p.96). Rosemary Tonks wrote much of her fiction in a villa on the island of Ischia near Naples where she spent several summer weeks every year from 1967 to 1975.

On being down, but not quite out, in Paris

More than 10 years ago I was living alone in Paris in a very ancient lodging house on the Île St Louis. I had come from Karachi, and was in a low physical condition after nearly a year in the heat getting over poliomyelitis.

The facts of my life, when you looked at them soberly, couldn't have been worse. I had only tropical clothes and little cash – just rent, food, and postage money. I didn't know a soul. I had managed to get a little room under the roof, with an annexe which had a cold water basin in it. There was a stone floor and a clean drab-mottled mat by the bed. A coarse cretonne cover fitted over the bed, with a bolster to match. The material was so rough that it gave you nettle-rash to touch it; I remember the background colour was a grimy pork pink.

I had to lay out money on a kerosene stove, a big expenditure. It was February when I installed it, and from then on it was a great joy and consolation to hear the tin kettle making sounds on top of it, while I sat at the only table and carefully wrote in the middle of the freezing little bedroom.

The poverty of that lodging-house was extreme. There was a spiral staircase going up through the building; you pushed on against chipped, black walls, as black as an ink-pot, and at the top you had to turn sideways to get yourself around the last bend. The lavatories were melodramatic, with dungeon lichen. A ramshackle door swung open and there was a Turkish earthenware well, with two ridged foot stands, one on either side. A touch on the chain brought foaming waters. The knack of getting out was quite simply to be acrobatic.

Everyone in the lodging-house, and for some way down the main street of the island, was a character, and they had a great deal of fulfilment from it. I was separated from them all by my quite obvious poor health, and this gave me the advantage of almost not being there, so that they could get on with their clowning. In the building itself, there was Raymonde – about 17 years old, dressed permanently in a broad-rimmed black hat, black vest, black shorts, and black top boots. She was either dusting with a sort of phosphorescent paint rag, inside a great dusty bush of spare dust, or else painting over the walls of a room with a gassy white emulsion that made you choke, and hanging French wallpaper with red patterns on it. There was 'Monsieur', tremendously motheaten, but somehow getting through his life satisfactorily by carrying a hammer and simply hitting anything that stuck out of the walls; the house was his and he had a perfect right to do so. There was the road-sweeper in his blue denims, who had a good, masculine, artisan's room on the important first floor; drinking went on in perfect silence in there, and he was regularly carried out, blue lips, dead limbs falling away from the body.

Outside in the street there was usually too much going on. There were processions of students carrying lanterns, or models from Pierre Balmain, unable to move because of their clothes, being more or less lifted into position by the old stone balustrade. There were fishermen down on the lower boulevard doing everything in slow motion, within their own time schemes. A professional guitarist would play melodiously in the rue St Louis. It was a compliment to the island that he was prepared to give himself to the street in this way.

Such a theatre-in-the-street gave you an illusion of well-being, and disguised the fact that life was as hard as nails....almost impossible. For example, to be given a torn note in my change was enough to make me sweat blood. I would hurry back to my room with the piece of rubbish, and mend it up so that it looked normal, and then, in a hang-dog way, rehearse how I would pass it on. I couldn't afford to make up the loss if it was refused.

The days went by in study, in writing a quarter-page stint of the novel I was working on (I worked at this for six years), in hovering outside the delicatessen and carefully getting ready the exact words and the exact money before going in. I ate cold ham and bread interminably. Sundays were a nightmare of solitude; everything shut. One Sunday a lodging-house on the left bank blew up; a man on the first floor had gassed himself, and someone upstairs had put a match to another kerosene stove.

The backdrop of the city of Paris helped to take the sting out of my situation; the elegance was impersonal, and life was grownup. This was a great relief after being so close to death. I couldn't stand anything homely, cajoling, or amateurish; didn't want to be embedded in clichés and silliness. And for the same reason, I didn't want to be a student and waste time doing amusing things.

There were days when I only left my room to walk for a bit in the late evening. One such evening I was coming back across *Pt Marie* from the right bank when I saw a man from the nineteenth century. I believe that certain conditions are necessary before an ordinary person can see a ghost. A tremendous inner pressure, or some suffering that has lowered your resistance, seem to be required. And the light was to he just right. The man I saw was absolutely solid and real. He wore a stove-pipe hat, pale waistcoat, frock coat, narrow trousers, pale gloves, and he looked at me as he passed. I was shaking with fright, and had to prop myself up against a dirty wall. It occurred to me that he could be an actor returning from a fancy dress party.

After that, there were evenings when I crept back to that bridge at exactly the same time, and hung about to see if he would reappear. On two other occasions I thought I saw him approaching in the distance, and as he came closer I saw that he was real – and at the sight, I instantly ran away, and got home the long way round, with my knees knocking together.

As the weather improved, I gave up ghost-watching. Attic windows were opened and one heard a great deal of music from other people's transistor radios. 'Monsieur' was revealed to be constructing a bathroom between two composition walls; it needed, and got, a good hammering every day. I slowly packed my objects into cardboard boxes. And one morning, putting all my strength together, I caught the 12.27 from the *Gare du Nord* for London, with exactly the same wondering, despondent feelings I used to have when going back to school.

[Published in *The Times*, 12 May 1976]